The CHERISHED TABLE

"It should come as no surprise that Lovina Eicher's latest cookbook, *The Cherished Table*, continues her tradition of offering up tasty and easy-to-make recipes for each meal of the day. An added bonus are the delightful stories and practical comments scattered throughout. *The Cherished Table* is sure to have your family cherishing mealtime around the family table."
—**Georgia Varozza**, author of *The Homestead Canning Cookbook*, *The Homestead Sourdough Cookbook*, and *The Homestyle Amish Kitchen Cookbook*

"Indulge in the delectable world of Amish cooking with *The Cherished Table* and savor a flavorsome journey featuring breakfast delights and comforting dinners. Lovina Eicher's home-style recipes will become staples in your everyday mealtime traditions and special occasions alike, making this cookbook a family treasure to pass on to the next generation."
—**Sherry Gore**, former editor-in-chief of *Cooking & Such Magazine* and author of *The Plain Choice* and *Me, Myself, and Pie*

"Step into the heart of Amish tradition and community with Lovina Eicher's delightful book *The Cherished Table*. Filled with mouthwatering recipes and heartwarming tales, this book invites you to experience the warmth of an Old Order Amish family. From stories about canning days to dishes for family gatherings, Eicher celebrates the joy of gathering around the table with loved ones. Whether you're a seasoned cook or a kitchen novice, this book will inspire you to create new memories and savor the simple pleasures of life shared with family and friends."
—**Suzanne Woods Fisher**, bestselling author of *Amish Proverbs: Words of Wisdom from the Simple Life*

"Simple ingredients, beautiful photography, personal notes, and tips for making each dish a success create an invitation to serve Lovina Eicher's recipes with love at your own kitchen table."
—**Marlin and Lisa Miller**, publishers of *Plain Values*

"Once again, Lovina Eicher has come up with a wonderful cookbook, beautifully photographed. It includes not only delicious recipes, but also the warm feeling of family, neighbors, and community. A great combination."
—**Elsie Kline**, garden and food editor of *Farming Magazine* and author of
The Farm Home Cookbook: Wholesome and Delicious Recipes from the Land

"Lovina Eicher had me at her Hash Brown Casserole, featuring one-quarter cup butter and whipping cream. Boy, do I love to drizzle butter, and there is so much butter-drizzling called for in the pages of *The Cherished Table*. Once I was in, I was all in, relishing the plenitude and variety of recipes and stories of Amish life by Eicher and her family members."
—**Lorilee Craker**, author of sixteen books, including the forthcoming
Eat Like a Heroine: Nourish and Flourish with Bookish Stars from Anne of Green Gables to Zora Neale Hurston, Money Secrets of the Amish, the
New York Times bestseller *Through the Storm* with Lynne Spears, and the
ECPA bestseller *My Journey to Heaven* with Marv Besteman

"After a lifetime in Amish country, we know how Amish kitchen cooking brings friends and family together. If you are interested in this special comfort-food tradition that is inspired by the garden and family farm, Lovina Eicher's new cookbook is for you!"
—**Dan and Mary Miller**, owners and board members of Der Dutchman
    Restaurants

"*The Cherished Table* offers more than just recipes—it's a heartwarming journey into the Amish way of life, where food is a celebration of family and community. Through over a hundred treasured recipes spanning breakfast to dessert, readers can explore the traditions and flavors that make Amish gatherings so special. With beautiful photographs and personal stories, Lovina Eicher invites us to embrace the values of faith, family, and fellowship, making this book a must-have for anyone seeking to create meaningful memories through food."
—**Susan Hougelman**, author of *Inside the Simple Life: Finding Inspiration among the Amish*

LOVINA EICHER'S AMISH KITCHEN

The CHERISHED TABLE

Recipes and Stories from an Amish Kitchen

Lovina Eicher

HERALD PRESS

Harrisonburg, Virginia

Herald Press
PO Box 866, Harrisonburg, Virginia 22803
www.HeraldPress.com

Library of Congress Cataloging-in-Publication Data
Names: Eicher, Lovina, author.
Title: The cherished table : recipes and stories from an Amish kitchen /
    Lovina Eicher.
Description: Harrisonburg : Herald Press, [2024] | Includes index.
Identifiers: LCCN 2024002833 (print) | LCCN 2024002834 (ebook) |
    ISBN 9781513813394 (paperback) | ISBN 9781513813400 (ebook)
Subjects: LCSH: Amish cooking. | Cooking, American. | BISAC: COOKING /
    Regional & Ethnic / Amish & Mennonite | COOKING / Comfort Food |
    LCGFT: Cookbooks.
Classification: LCC TX721 .E3523 2024 (print) | LCC TX721 (ebook) |
    DDC 641.5/66--dc23/eng/20240212
LC record available at https://lccn.loc.gov/2024002833
LC ebook record available at https://lccn.loc.gov/2024002834

THE CHERISHED TABLE
© 2024 by Herald Press, Harrisonburg, Virginia 22803. 800-245-7894.
    All rights reserved.
Library of Congress Control Number: 2024002833
International Standard Book Number: 978-1-5138-1339-4 (paperback);
    978-1-5138-1340-0 (ebook)
Printed in United States of America
Cover and interior design by Merrill Miller
Cover and interior photos by Jennifer Beachy; additional interior photos by
    Grant Beachy and Getty Images
Food styling by Jennifer Beachy

28 27 26 25 24   10 9 8 7 6 5 4 3 2 1

To my family, with whom I have shared many cherished meals around our kitchen table. May God always bless our family.

CONTENTS

INTRODUCTION

*W*elcome to my family table!

I began cooking and baking as a young girl growing up in Indiana. When I was a teenager, my mother, Elizabeth Coblenz, started penning a food column. After her unexpected death over a decade later, I took over writing the column. I eventually went on to write several cookbooks, including *Amish Family Recipes* and *The Essential Amish Cookbook*. In 2014, my column was renamed Lovina's Amish Kitchen, and it is published in newspapers across the United States and on a Facebook page. This year, I'm delighted to be celebrating the tenth anniversary of Lovina's Amish Kitchen, and over twenty years authoring a cooking column.

As readers of the column may know, our family has experienced many changes over the years. My husband Joe and I have eight adult children. Through the thirty-plus years of our marriage, times haven't always been easy. When the children were young and needed shoes, boots, coats, and clothes, providing for eight growing children could be hard on the wallet. There were a few times when Joe didn't have full-time work or was laid off, and we had a hard time not knowing whether we would make it financially. This struggle brought us closer to God—we knew that if we trusted in him, God would provide. God always did. It also helped to have our own chickens for eggs, a cow for milk, and a garden for produce, and to raise and butcher our own poultry, beef, and pork. Joe loves to fish and hunt, so that filled our freezer with venison and fish as well. In these pages, you'll find stories written by me and several family members about work done around the farm and kitchen and memories from our home and community.

Though Joe and I have fewer children living at home today, our family table is often overflowing with loved ones. Several of our children are married and have children of their own. We welcomed two new grandbabies in the last year, bringing the total to twelve grandchildren. Sadly, in 2020, our son-in-law Mose passed away after a car accident. He and our daughter Susan had been married for four years and had two children. We continue to mourn his loss. And yet we are able to thank God for unexpected blessings. As Susan shares on page 225, "God had plans for our future that we never thought would be possible." Susan met Ervin, who was also widowed and had three children, and they married in late 2022. Their family expanded to eight with the birth of Ervin Jay Yoder Jr. the next year. Everyone, including Ervin Jay's five older siblings, was very eager to meet him. As grandparents, Joe and I greatly enjoy spending time with all our grandchildren.

When our children were all young and still in our care, preparing meals for a family of ten could be a challenge. But this new family season brings new dilemmas. As the house empties and the meals have to be smaller in size, I really have to teach myself not to make too much food. Downsizing is hard for me. All my recipes were designed for big family meals—often with the goal of having leftovers for another meal. But it's also fun to share recipes with the grandchildren and try new dishes from our children-in-law and their extended families.

In this book, I've collected cherished favorites, both new ones and those that are tried and true. This cookbook is organized around moments of the day and year. You'll find a variety of dishes for many occasions and seasons—whether a quick yet filling weekend breakfast, a hearty soup for a wintry night, a delicious plan for all that homegrown (or store-bought) zucchini and rhubarb, or a casserole or cake to take to friends or family. You'll also find dishes that work well with young cooks, or at least hungry ones, as well as recipes to feed a crowd. We often cook food for dozens; feel free to reduce the measurements if you're anticipating a smaller crowd.

No matter the size of your family or your season of life, I invite you to gather your loved ones and make these recipes part of your own cherished table.

A NOTE ON INGREDIENTS

The recipes draw on pantry basics like flour, sugar, butter, spices, and shortening. My family likes a variety of cheeses, and many of the dishes that call for cheese can easily substitute a similar kind for another. We always have meat on hand in the freezer, and our garden provides produce to prepare fresh as well as to can and freeze. But store-bought goods can easily be substituted.

I buy my flour and other pantry items in bulk. When I buy sugar in bulk, the bags of powdered sugar, also known as confectioners' sugar, are labeled as "powdered sugar." Well, I didn't realize that at least one of my daughters (I won't name names) didn't know that confectioners' sugar and powdered sugar are the same thing. In my last cookbook, the recipes called for "confectioners' sugar." When my daughter followed the recipe for whoopie pies, she figured that confectioners' sugar was just another word for regular, granulated (white) sugar—that is, until she tasted the results! So to avoid confusion, all the recipes in this book that use confectioners'/powdered sugar call for powdered sugar.

Several recipes call for Clear Jel, which is a modified cornstarch made for thickening. It is often used in fruit pie fillings and other fillings or sauces. There are two kinds of Clear Jel: instant (or no-cook) and regular (cooking required). Instant Clear Jel does not require heat to thicken, but regular Clear Jel does. Both regular and instant Clear Jel are often available in bulk food stores.

Finally, there are certain brands that I tend to always use, such as Miracle Whip salad dressing, Velveeta, and Ritz crackers. In the recipes, these are usually referred to generically—whipped salad dressing, process cheese spread, and round buttery crackers, for example. That way you can choose accordingly without having to purchase a specific brand.

Starting Out
EGGS AND OTHER BREAKFAST DISHES

BAKED VEGGIE OMELET

Makes 8 servings

This is a tasty one-dish breakfast and an easy way to start your day with some vegetables. When we keep chickens, we like the ISA Brown and Rhode Island Red chickens for eggs. We like to start new chickens every two or three years.

2 cups shredded Monterey Jack cheese

1 medium green pepper, seeded and chopped

**1 (4-ounce) can mushroom stems and pieces, drained;
    or 1 cup sliced fresh mushrooms**

1 medium onion, chopped

½ cup cubed fully cooked ham

12 eggs

½ cup milk

1 teaspoon hot pepper sauce

¼ teaspoon salt

Dash pepper

In a greased 13 x 9-inch baking dish, layer half the cheese, green pepper, mushrooms, onion, and ham. Repeat layers. In a bowl, beat together the eggs, milk, hot pepper sauce, salt, and pepper. Pour over vegetable mixture. Bake, uncovered, at 350°F for 25 to 30 minutes, or until a knife inserted near the center comes out clean.

FARMER'S OMELET

Makes 12 to 14 servings

Sometimes instead of making one big omelet for the family, we make individual omelets using two or three eggs per person. Each person can select the toppings they want in their omelet. But this large one-pan omelet offers a quick and easy way to serve a crowd.

1½ cups chopped onion

3 tablespoons canola or olive oil

4 cups peeled, diced potatoes, cooked

10 bacon strips, cooked and crumbled

½ cup diced ham

½ cup dried beef (also known as chipped beef), chopped

12 eggs

3 tablespoons minced fresh parsley

2 teaspoons paprika

1 teaspoon salt

½ teaspoon pepper

In a large skillet over medium heat, cook onion in oil until tender. Add cooked potatoes, bacon, ham, and beef; heat through. In a large bowl, beat eggs. Stir in parsley, paprika, salt, and pepper. Add in meat mixture, stirring gently. Pour into a greased 13 x 9-inch baking dish. Bake, uncovered, at 400°F for 20 to 30 minutes.

BREAKFAST SKILLET

Makes 10 servings

This is a great breakfast to pull together using our home-raised eggs, meat from the freezer, and fresh vegetables from our garden. We try to grow enough potatoes and onions to store for most of the winter. Many people in our family love sprinkling hot peppers over top of this dish.

1 pound bacon

1 pound pork sausage

1½ cups shredded cooked potatoes

¼ cup chopped onion

8 eggs

2 tablespoons milk

2 tablespoons minced fresh parsley

¼ teaspoon salt

½ cup shredded cheese (such as cheddar, Swiss, or pepper jack)

1 green bell pepper, seeded and chopped

1 small tomato, chopped

Cut bacon into small pieces and fry in a large skillet. Remove bacon from pan and discard grease. In the same skillet, brown and crumble sausage until fully cooked. Remove sausage, retaining drippings. Cook potatoes and onions in the drippings until potatoes are soft.

In a separate bowl, beat eggs, milk, parsley, and salt. Pour egg mixture over potato mixture in the warm skillet. Add cooked bacon and sausage. Cook over medium heat, stirring, until eggs are set. Sprinkle with cheese. Cover skillet for 1 to 2 minutes, or until the cheese is melted. Remove from heat and top with bell peppers and tomatoes.

BACON AND EGG LASAGNA

Makes 12 servings

Some people in our family don't care for Swiss cheese, so sometimes I change it to Colby cheese, our family's overall favorite. This recipe calls for a dozen hard-cooked eggs: Place the eggs in a large saucepan, cover with water, and bring to a boil. Boil, uncovered, for two minutes. Then turn off the heat and let them sit, still covered, for eleven minutes. Drain the hot water and run cold water over the eggs.

1 pound bacon

1 large onion, chopped

⅓ cup all-purpose flour

¾ teaspoon salt

¼ teaspoon pepper

4 cups milk

9 lasagna noodles, cooked

12 hard-cooked eggs, sliced

2 cups shredded Swiss cheese

⅓ cup grated Parmesan cheese

2 tablespoons minced fresh parsley

Cook and crumble bacon. Reserve ⅓ cup of the drippings and use to sauté onions until tender. Stir in flour, salt, and pepper until blended. Gradually add the milk. Bring to a simmer and stir for 2 minutes. Spread ½ cup white sauce into the bottom of a 13 x 9-inch greased baking pan. Layer with three lasagna noodles and one-third of the eggs, crumbled bacon, cheese, and white sauce. Repeat layers twice. Sprinkle with parsley. Bake, uncovered, at 350°F for 35 to 40 minutes. Let stand for 15 minutes before serving.

OVERNIGHT BREAKFAST CASSEROLE

Makes 10 to 12 servings

Since you can make it the night before, this recipe is convenient to supply a meal on a busy morning when I don't have time to make anything. I sometimes make it to serve company in the morning, or to take along somewhere as a carry-in dish.

8 tablespoons (1 stick) butter, divided

4 tablespoons all-purpose flour

3 cups milk

½ teaspoon salt

¼ teaspoon pepper

1½ cups (12 ounces) process cheese spread, cubed

⅓ cup chopped onion

12 eggs, beaten

1 pound sausage, browned, or ham, cubed

1 cup sliced fresh mushrooms (optional)

6 potatoes, peeled and shredded

2 cups crushed cornflakes

To make cheese sauce: In a medium saucepan, melt 3 tablespoons butter, blend in flour, and cook for 1 minute. Gradually stir in milk; cook until thickened. Add salt, pepper, and cheese spread; stir until melted.

In a large skillet over medium heat, sauté onion in 3 additional tablespoons of butter; add eggs, and cook until set. Stir in meat, mushrooms (if using), and prepared cheese sauce. Put shredded potatoes in the bottom of a greased 13 x 9-inch baking pan. Add egg mixture. Refrigerate at least 8 hours or overnight.

Melt the remaining 2 tablespoons butter and stir into the crushed cornflakes. Sprinkle cornflake mixture over top of the casserole. Bake at 350°F for 30 minutes.

HASH BROWN CASSEROLE

Makes 6 servings

Our family loves any casserole with hash browns in it. Potatoes are a favorite around here and can be part of almost any meal. We grow our own potatoes and shred them fresh instead of buying them frozen. This makes a great dish for potlucks or to take to households in need.

3 cups shredded hash brown potatoes, thawed if using frozen

¼ cup (½ stick) butter, melted and divided

1 cup shredded pepper jack cheese

1 cup shredded Swiss cheese

1 cup diced fully cooked ham or sausage, browned

2 eggs

½ cup whipping cream

¼ teaspoon seasoned salt

Press hash browns between paper towels to remove excess moisture. Grease a 9-inch pie plate with 2 teaspoons of the melted butter. Press hash browns onto the bottom and up the sides of the pie plate. Drizzle with the remaining 8 teaspoons butter. Bake, uncovered, at 425°F for 20 to 25 minutes, or until the edges are browned. Combine cheeses and ham or sausage; spoon into the baked crust. In a bowl, beat the eggs, whipping cream, and seasoned salt; pour over cheese and meat mixture.

Reduce the heat to 350°F. Bake, uncovered, for 20 to 25 minutes, or until a knife inserted near the center comes out clean. Let stand for 10 minutes before cutting into wedges.

DAIRY COWS

As a young girl at home, I helped milk our stable of around twelve to fourteen cows in the morning and evening. I started helping when I was around seven or eight years old. At first I would milk one side of the cow and my sister the other. Finally my arms toughened up to milk a cow alone. Each child started on the easiest milking cows. Dad and my brothers would always milk the young cows until they were tame enough for us girls to milk them. Some milked really easily and some were harder milkers who would stomp and sometimes kick. To keep certain cows from kicking, we would use a back clamp, which slips over the back of the cow and down on both sides, depressing muscles that control kicking and immobilizing the cow's rear legs without pain or injury. And then there was Daisy. I believe she was the hardest milking cow there ever was. It required all your muscles to squeeze the milk from her. Needless to say, she was always the last cow to be milked!

Probably the most annoying thing about milking a cow was its tail. The cow would swish it back and forth and into our face as we sat on milk stools milking them. Dad would wear a hat so they couldn't hit his face. My sisters and I would tie up the tails with baler twine until we were done. Dad always warned us to not forget to untie their tails before turning them out of their cow stanchions.

We strained the fresh milk through a filter and then ran it into the milk cans. We then submerged the cans in cold water and pumped fresh water over the cans for several hours to keep them chilled until the next morning when the milkman came. It was tricky in the heat of the summer because the water would need to be changed out more often.

When Joe and I were first married we had a milk cow. Joe would milk it before he went to work every morning and then again after he came home. A milkman stopped by every morning to pick up our excess milk. We had two stainless steel milk cans with our number painted on the side so the milkman knew which cans belonged to us. It also let the milk company know whom to pay for the milk. Our milk was grade B and went to a cheese company. We could order horns of cheese from the milkman, and the cost would be deducted from our milk check. We got a milk check every two weeks, which really helped us as a young couple starting out on a mini farm.

Our children loved taking their cups out to Joe while he milked our cow, Bessie. He would squirt milk in their cups, and they would drink the warm milk. I don't think I could drink milk warm, but the barn kittens sure loved it when Joe filled their dish with milk at each milking!

We don't keep a cow today; we get our milk from the store or our neighbors. Where we live in Michigan, there aren't ways to sell the excess milk. But some families share a milk cow, and some will make butter, cheese, and cottage cheese.

—Lovina

BREAKFAST HASH WITH TOMATO GRAVY

Makes 6 to 8 servings

I was never fond of tomato gravy (although I love tomatoes), but Joe and some of the children love to eat this for breakfast once in a while. The hash can also be served with browned sausage.

Tomato gravy
4 cups tomato juice
1 cup milk
2 tablespoons all-purpose flour
Salt and black pepper, to taste

Breakfast hash
6 to 8 slices bread, toasted
6 to 8 hard-cooked eggs

Prepare the tomato gravy: In a medium nonaluminum saucepan, bring the tomato juice to a boil. Whisk together the milk and flour in a small bowl. Slowly add the flour mixture to the tomato juice, whisking constantly. Return to a boil and cook until the tomato gravy is slightly thickened. Stir in salt and pepper. Remove from heat.

Assemble hash: Crumble toasted bread on a plate. Top with a warm hard-cooked egg, diced or whole. Cover with tomato gravy.

OATMEAL PANCAKES

Makes 12 to 14 pancakes

This is a healthier way of making pancakes and is great for those who love oatmeal for breakfast.

1½ cups rolled oats
2 cups milk
½ cup all-purpose flour
1 tablespoon granulated sugar
1 teaspoon baking soda
1 teaspoon salt
2 eggs, beaten
1 tablespoon oil, plus additional for the griddle

Mix oats and milk in a large bowl; add flour and beat together with a whisk. Mix in the remaining ingredients (sugar through oil). Heat a griddle over medium-high heat and add a little oil to keep the pancakes from sticking. Ladle the batter evenly into pancakes on the hot griddle. Cook pancakes a few minutes on each side until both sides are brown.

GERMAN OVEN PANCAKE

Makes one 8-inch pancake

This is an easy way to make pancakes and a nice change for breakfast. The pancake should puff up while baking, and then quickly deflate after it's removed from the oven. You can also sprinkle chocolate chips and pour maple syrup on top before serving.

1 egg, at room temperature
⅓ cup milk, at room temperature
1 tablespoon butter, melted
1 teaspoon vanilla extract
1 tablespoon granulated sugar
Dash salt
⅓ cup all-purpose flour
Shortening, for greasing the pan
Powdered sugar, for serving

Preheat the oven to 425°F and heat an oven-proof 8-inch skillet in it for 10 minutes. Whisk together egg, milk, butter, vanilla, sugar, and salt in a medium bowl. Whisk in flour to make a smooth batter. Remove the hot skillet from the oven, carefully brush it with shortening, pour in batter, and return to the oven for 5 minutes. Reduce heat to 350°F and bake the pancake 8 to 10 minutes more. Sprinkle with powdered sugar to serve.

BAKED FRENCH TOAST

Serves 4 to 6

We usually prefer this version over pan-fried French toast—it's moist yet crunchy and has great flavor. When daughter Susan still lived at home, she always made this for breakfast, and the younger ones loved it. It tastes delicious served with maple syrup.

In years past, son-in-law Tim and daughter Elizabeth have gathered sap from their maple trees with the horse and wagon. The bags are emptied into the buckets on the wagon, then taken to the cooker to cook down, which takes hours and hours. It takes around thirty gallons of sap to cook down to one gallon of maple syrup. Our late son-in-law, Mose, also used to tap our trees for maple sap and cook it down to syrup for our year's supply. He loved to pour the hot, fresh syrup over vanilla ice cream.

1 cup packed brown sugar

½ cup (1 stick) butter

2 tablespoons light corn syrup

12 bread slices

½ cup granulated sugar

1 teaspoon ground cinnamon

6 eggs

1½ cups milk

1 teaspoon vanilla extract

In a heavy-bottomed saucepan, combine the brown sugar, butter, and corn syrup. Heat the ingredients over medium-high heat, stirring frequently. When the mixture reaches a boil, remove it from the heat and pour it into the bottom of a 13 x 9-inch glass baking pan.

Layer the bread slices into the glass pan and sprinkle with the sugar and the cinnamon. In a large bowl, whisk the eggs, milk, and vanilla together until smooth and evenly combined. Pour the egg mixture over the bread. Bake at 350°F for 30 to 35 minutes until puffed and golden.

CINNAMON BREAKFAST BALLS

Makes 6 servings (2½ dozen)

This is a delightful breakfast snack to enjoy with a cup of coffee in the morning. The grandchildren love eating them with milk.

1⅓ cups all-purpose flour

1 cup crispy rice cereal, coarsely crushed

2 tablespoons plus ½ cup granulated sugar, divided

3 teaspoons baking powder

½ teaspoon salt

¼ cup butter-flavored shortening

½ cup milk

1 teaspoon ground cinnamon

¼ cup (½ stick) butter, melted

In a bowl, combine the flour, crushed crispy rice cereal, 2 tablespoons sugar, baking powder, and salt. Cut in shortening using a pastry blender or your fingers until the mixture resembles coarse crumbs. Stir in milk just until moistened. Shape the dough into 1-inch balls. In a separate bowl, combine cinnamon and remaining ½ cup sugar. Dip dough balls in melted butter, then roll in cinnamon-sugar mixture. Arrange balls in a single layer in a greased 8-inch round baking pan. Bake at 425°F for 15 to 18 minutes, or until a toothpick inserted near the center comes out clean.

DANISH BREAKFAST BARS

Makes 24 to 30 bars

These are delicious breakfast bars. You can use the pie filling of your choice (see Homemade Fruit Pie Filling on p. 112). I like to try a variety of flavors and often use whatever fruit is in season.

4 eggs
1 cup (2 sticks) butter
2 cups granulated sugar
½ teaspoon salt
4 cups all-purpose flour
1½ teaspoons baking powder
1 teaspoon vanilla extract
1 quart (4 cups) Homemade Fruit Pie Filling (p. 112), warmed

Glaze
½ cup (1 stick) butter
3 tablespoon milk
3 cups powdered sugar
1 teaspoon vanilla extract

Make the bars: In a large bowl, mix together eggs, butter, granulated sugar, and salt until creamy. Add flour, baking powder, and vanilla. The batter will be thick. Spread about three-quarters of the batter on the bottom of a 15 x 10-inch rimmed baking sheet. Spread warm pie filling on top. Dab the remaining dough on top of filling. Bake at 350°F for 15 to 20 minutes. Do not overbake. When the dough is golden brown, it's ready.

Prepare the glaze: Melt butter in a saucepan. Add milk and stir occasionally. Once the mixture is hot, add powdered sugar and vanilla. Mix together. Glaze the bars while still warm.

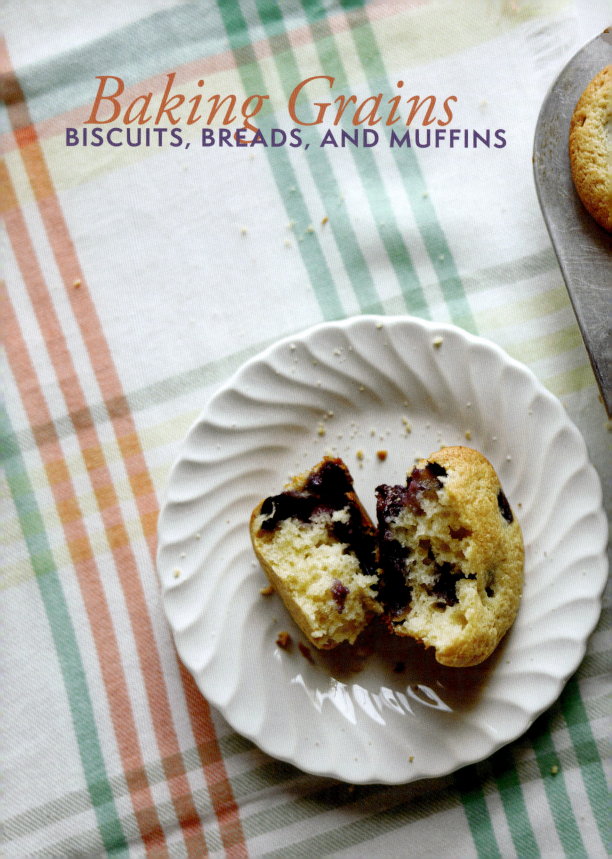

Baking Grains
BISCUITS, BREADS, AND MUFFINS

SOFT DINNER ROLLS

Makes 32 rolls

These are nice served warm with butter as a snack or with a full-course meal. They are also handy cut in half and used to make small sandwiches. We enjoy making tomato sandwiches by spreading mayo on the bread and adding sliced fresh tomatoes from the garden. This recipe calls for scalded milk: heat milk to just below boiling, then cool to room temperature.

1 cup milk, scalded

½ cup (1 stick) butter, melted

2 eggs, beaten

1 cup warm water

¾ cup granulated sugar

2 tablespoons yeast (may measure out from three 1¼-ounce packages)

2 teaspoons salt

6 cups bread flour, plus additional for kneading

Mix together all ingredients in a large bowl until it forms a rough dough, then turn out onto a floured counter and knead for 10 minutes. Cover lightly with a towel and let rise for 1 hour. Divide dough in half. Continue dividing each portion in half until you have 32 even pieces. Shape each piece into a rounded roll and place them on greased baking sheets just close enough to be touching slightly. Cover rolls lightly with a kitchen towel and let rise until doubled in bulk. Bake in a preheated 350°F oven for 20 to 25 minutes.

ICEBOX BUTTERHORNS

Makes 2 dozen

These pastries are sometimes served at weddings instead of homemade bread or dinner rolls. These are also good to serve for a holiday dinner or a Sunday home-cooked meal. This recipe dates back from the days of using iceboxes—but today we use a propane-powered refrigerator.

1 (1¼-ounce) package active dry yeast
2 tablespoons warm water (110°F to 115°F)
2 cups warm milk (110°F to 115°F)
½ cup granulated sugar
1 egg, beaten
1 teaspoon salt
6 cups all-purpose flour, divided
¾ cup (1½ sticks) butter, melted
Additional melted butter

In a large mixing bowl, dissolve yeast in warm water. Add warm milk, sugar, egg, salt, and 3 cups flour; beat until smooth. Beat in melted butter and remaining 3 cups flour (dough will be slightly sticky). Do not knead. Place in a greased bowl. Cover and refrigerate for 8 hours or overnight.

Punch dough down and divide in half. On a floured surface, use a rolling pin to roll each half into a twelve-inch circle. Cut each circle into 12 pie-shaped wedges. Beginning at the wide end, roll up each wedge. Place rolls, point side down, 2 inches apart on greased baking sheets. Cover and let rise in a warm place until doubled, about 1 hour. Bake at 350°F for 15 to 20 minutes, or until golden brown. Immediately brush tops with melted butter.

SOURDOUGH BREAD AND STARTER

Makes 3 loaves

I used to make sourdough bread all the time when the girls were younger because it was an easy bread for them to bake alongside me. We would also make cinnamon rolls with this recipe. If you make cinnamon rolls, just roll the dough out as you would for other cinnamon roll recipes and then add the butter and cinnamon-sugar filling (see the instructions for Speedy Cinnamon Rolls on p. 58).

1 cup sourdough starter (see p. 49)

1½ cups warm water (105°F to 115°F)

½ cup olive oil

6 cups bread flour

2 tablespoons granulated sugar

1 teaspoon salt

1 tablespoon butter, melted

Combine the sourdough starter, warm water, oil, flour, sugar, and salt in a large bowl. Stir together to make a dough. Form the dough into a ball. Grease another large bowl. Put the dough ball in the bowl and turn to coat. Cover with wax paper, then let the dough stand overnight or at least 8 hours. Do not refrigerate.

The next morning (or 8 hours later), punch the dough down and divide it into thirds. Knead each portion on a floured surface 8 to 10 times. Shape each piece into a small loaf. Grease three 8½ x 4½ x 2½-inch loaf pans and turn each loaf over in the pans to coat. Cover with wax paper and let rise in the pans until the dough is just above the rims of the pans, 4 to 5 hours.

Bake the bread in an oven preheated to 350°F until the crust is nice and golden brown, 30 to 35 minutes. Remove from the oven and brush each loaf with 1 tablespoon melted butter. Remove loaves from pans and let cool on wire racks.

SOURDOUGH STARTER

If you already have starter made, just skip to the "starter feed" section of the instructions. If not, begin from scratch. Either way, tending sourdough starter takes some time, trial, and error to get it right, but once you do, it is definitely worthwhile! When the girls were younger, they enjoyed feeding the starter for me.

Starter
3 packages (1¼-ounce each) active dry yeast
1 cup warm water (105°F to 115°F)

Starter feed
¾ cup granulated sugar
3 tablespoons instant potato flakes
1 cup warm water (105°F to 115°F)

Make the starter: Mix the yeast and warm water in a small bowl. Put into a plastic container, seal, and refrigerate for 3 to 5 days. The starter will then be ready to be "fed."

Make the starter feed: Combine the sugar, instant potatoes, and water in a small bowl and stir it into the starter. Cover loosely (to allow some pressure to escape as the gas builds) and let stand at room temperature for 5 to 12 hours. The mixture will be bubbly.

Take out 1 cup of starter to make bread and loosely cover the remaining starter and return it to the refrigerator. Feed again after 3 to 5 days. If not making bread after feeding the starter, throw away 1 cup to avoid depleting the starter.

Note: After you have fed the starter and when you store it, do not seal the container tightly. I store mine in a gallon-sized resealable plastic bag and only zip it loosely closed.

MYSTERY BISCUITS

Makes 12 biscuits

The "mystery" in these biscuits is the mayonnaise (or whipped salad dressing), which gives them a very moist flavor, although I always use Miracle Whip instead of mayonnaise. We always enjoy these with homemade sausage gravy. One of my nieces uses this recipe for her pizza crust.

2 cups all-purpose flour
1 tablespoon baking powder
1 teaspoon salt
¼ cup mayonnaise or whipped salad dressing
1 cup milk
1 teaspoon granulated sugar

Preheat the oven to 375°F. Grease a baking sheet or 12 muffin cups and set aside. In a large bowl, combine the flour, baking powder, and salt. Blend in the mayonnaise, milk, and sugar until the mixture is creamy. Drop by tablespoonfuls onto the prepared baking sheet or fill the muffin cups two-thirds full. Bake until golden brown, 18 to 20 minutes.

SHOPPING AND FOOD PLANNING

I like shopping at bulk food stores and stocking up on flour, sugars, and such. I always buy my bread flour in fifty-pound bags, and our cheese by the horn (essentially, a multipound loaf of cheese). Even though my supply list grows smaller because we have fewer people living at home, our family of twenty-eight (at last count) still comes home often for a meal. I usually peel and chop ten pounds of potatoes for mashed potatoes when they come. If we grill chicken, it takes around twenty pounds, so I still need to have plenty on hand. I love it when they all come home and I can cook for all of them. I enjoy hearing them say they were hungry for Mom's cooking again. Family time together is important!

Packing lunches can be a challenge as well. You want to make sure the lunches don't grow tiresome. Eating the same thing over and over can get old pretty fast. I appreciate when Joe or my children tell me what they like or tell me what food sounds good to them in a certain week. Joe worked in factories for almost twenty-four years, and they usually had a microwave to heat up food. Now he works at a metal and truss shop owned by an Amish couple, so there isn't a microwave. There is a stove and oven, however, so the workers do have a way to heat up their food. Joe mostly takes leftovers from the night before for his lunch.

My daughters always packed their own lunches when they lived at home. My sons work construction right now and they pack their lunches, but they don't have any way to heat up the food. Fortunately, they don't mind cold food when they are hungry. Joseph says it is better to eat his food cold and have a variety than to have a sandwich every day.

When I'm making packed lunches, I will often fill a thermos with hot soup or something else that fits, and it stays pretty warm that way. Other foods the boys like in their lunches are frozen peaches (a bag of frozen peaches works as an ice pack and yet will be thawed by lunchtime), apples, grapes, cookies, pie, bars, peanuts, oranges, and crackers with a cheese ball or a salad. Two favorite treats to tuck in are Pumpkin Whoopie Pies (p. 174) and Lunchroom Brownies (p. 150).

—*Lovina*

YEASTED PIZZA DOUGH

Makes one 14- to 16-inch pizza

I like to try different kinds of pizza dough. There are several recipes that I use. I like this crust because the yeast makes it puff up more than crusts without yeast. This one makes a 14- to 16-inch pizza depending on how thick you prefer your crust. We like to put a lot of toppings on our pizza, such as pepperoni, bacon, green bell peppers, olives, mushrooms, banana peppers, hot peppers, and so on. You can find my recipe for Pizza Sauce on page 97.

Dough

1 package (1¼-ounce) active dry yeast

1 cup warm water (110°F to 115°F)

¼ cup canola or vegetable oil

1 teaspoon granulated sugar

1 teaspoon salt

3 cups all-purpose or bread flour, divided

Toppings

1 pint pizza sauce (see p. 97 for a recipe option)

4 to 5 cups shredded mozzarella cheese

1 pound ground sausage or beef, cooked and drained

1 to 2 cups sliced vegetables (such as peppers, onions, mushrooms) and other toppings of your choice

Preheat oven to 350°F.

Dissolve the yeast in warm water. Add oil, sugar, and salt. Mix thoroughly. Add half the flour and beat until there are no lumps. Gradually add remaining flour. Knead dough for 5 minutes. Press out onto a 14- or 16-inch pizza pan (use a 14-inch pan if you prefer a thicker crust). Prebake crust at 350°F for 10 minutes. Spread pizza sauce over dough and top with cheese and meat. Add other additional toppings, if desired. Bake an additional 20 minutes at 350°F, or until crust is golden brown.

QUICK BAKING MIX

This is perfect to have on hand to make Deep Dish Taco Squares (p. 198). It's also great for mixing quick biscuits or pancakes.

8 cups all-purpose flour
2 teaspoons salt
⅓ cup baking powder
1 cup shortening or butter (2 sticks)

Sift dry ingredients; cut in shortening. Blend until mixture resembles coarse meal. Store in an airtight container at room temperature for up to 3 months.

For biscuits: Combine 1 cup baking mix with ⅓ cup milk. Mix lightly, then turn out onto a floured surface and roll out to 1 inch thick. Cut into biscuits. Place on a greased baking sheet and bake at 350°F for 15 to 20 minutes, or until golden brown. Makes 6 biscuits.

For pancakes: Combine 2 cups baking mix with 2 tablespoons granulated sugar, 2 cups milk, and 2 beaten eggs. Whisk together and ladle pancake batter onto a hot skillet. Cook pancakes a few minutes on each side until both sides are browned. Makes 12 to 14 pancakes.

FRIED GARLIC TOAST

Makes 4 to 6 servings

We usually make garlic bread in the oven. When it's just a few of us at home for supper, though, we do it this way, and preferably with homemade bread. We love to have garlic toast with spaghetti and meatballs.

1 to 2 tablespoons butter
¼ teaspoon garlic powder
6 slices white or wheat bread, halved

Melt butter over low heat in a large skillet. Sprinkle garlic powder over melted butter. Fry bread in the garlic butter until golden brown on both sides.

SPEEDY CINNAMON ROLLS

Makes about 2 dozen rolls

These cinnamon rolls don't require as much time to rise, which earns them the name "speedy." Our children like a generous amount of frosting on their cinnamon rolls. These rolls go great with a cup of coffee while our usual Saturday morning breakfast is being prepared. These are also nice to enjoy with friends or family at a coffee break.

6½ cups bread flour, divided

2 cups warm water (105°F to 115°F)

½ cup granulated sugar

4½ teaspoons (2 packages, 1¼-ounce each) active dry yeast

1 tablespoon salt

2 eggs, beaten

⅓ cup lard or shortening

6 tablespoons butter, softened

1 cup packed brown sugar, divided

1 tablespoon ground cinnamon, divided

In a large bowl, combine 2 cups bread flour with the warm water, granulated sugar, yeast, and salt. Beat the mixture for 2 minutes with a wooden spoon, then add the eggs and lard. Stir until well blended. Gradually add the remaining 4½ cups bread flour and stir until a firm dough is formed. Cover the bowl with a clean kitchen towel and set it in a warm area to rest for 20 minutes.

After the dough has rested, punch it down, divide it in half, and form two balls. On a floured surface, roll one ball of dough out as thinly as possible. Brush half the softened butter evenly over the dough, then sprinkle with half the brown sugar and half the cinnamon. Roll the dough up starting from the longer side and pinch the edges closed. Using a sharp serrated knife, cut the roll into slices ½ to ¾ inch thick. Place slices half an inch apart in a greased 13 x 9-inch baking pan. Repeat with the remaining ball of dough and the remaining butter, brown sugar, and cinnamon, placing the second set of rolls on a separate greased pan. Cover the rolls with paper towels or clean kitchen towels, place the pans in a warm area, and allow to rise for about 45 minutes, or until doubled in size.

While the rolls are rising, preheat the oven to 350°F. Bake the rolls for 15 to 20 minutes, until they are golden brown. Allow the rolls to cool on wire racks for 15 minutes. If desired, you may frost the rolls with your favorite frosting before serving. See Decorator's Cream Cheese Frosting (p. 111) for one option.

PEANUT BUTTER MINI MUFFINS

Makes 3 dozen mini muffins

These sweet mini muffins are a family favorite. My grandchildren think they are cute and love the chocolate candies sprinkled on top. After son-in-law Tim and daughter Elizabeth's children sampled these during one of the photography sessions for this book, they asked Elizabeth to make them again the very next day! Granddaughter Abigail also asked to share them with her class on her birthday.

These can also be made in a regular-sized muffin pan: Divide batter evenly among a regular 12-cup muffin tin and bake for 22 to 24 minutes.

⅓ cup creamy peanut butter

¼ cup (½ stick) butter, softened

¼ cup granulated sugar

¼ cup firmly packed light brown sugar

1 large egg

¾ cup buttermilk

3 tablespoons canola or vegetable oil

¾ teaspoon vanilla extract

1½ cups all-purpose flour

¾ teaspoon baking powder

½ teaspoon baking soda

½ teaspoon salt

1¼ cups mini candy-coated chocolate pieces, divided

Chocolate Glaze

2 (1-ounce) squares semisweet chocolate

1 tablespoon butter

Preheat the oven to 350°F. Lightly grease 36 (1¼-inch) mini muffin cups or line with paper or foil liners; set pan aside.

In a large bowl, cream together peanut butter, butter, and sugars until light and fluffy; beat in egg. Beat in buttermilk, oil, and vanilla.

In medium bowl, combine flour, baking powder, baking soda, and salt; gradually blend into creamed mixture. Divide batter evenly among prepared muffin cups. Sprinkle batter evenly with ¾ cup candy-coated chocolate pieces. Bake mini muffins for 15 to 17 minutes, or until a toothpick inserted in the center of one of the muffins comes out clean. Cool completely on wire racks.

Prepare chocolate glaze: Melt chocolate and butter on top of a double boiler over hot water. Stir until smooth; let cool slightly. Pour glaze into a resealable plastic sandwich bag. Cut a tiny piece off one corner of the bag (no more than an ⅛ inch). Drizzle glaze over muffins. Decorate with remaining ½ cup candy-coated chocolate pieces. Store leftover mini muffins in a tightly sealed container.

BERRY CREAM CHEESE MUFFINS

Makes 18 muffins

We make these most often with blueberries. I used to not care for blueberries that much, so I never made recipes with blueberries. I think it was thanks to my friend Ruth bringing us several dishes with blueberries in them that I discovered that my kids love blueberries. If using frozen berries, there is no need to thaw them first.

1 cup (2 sticks) butter, softened

1 (8-ounce) package cream cheese, softened

1½ cups granulated sugar

1½ teaspoons vanilla extract

4 large eggs

2 cups all-purpose flour

1½ teaspoons baking powder

½ teaspoon salt

2 cups fresh or frozen cranberries, blueberries, or raspberries, dusted with 2 tablespoons all-purpose flour

1½ cups pecan or walnuts, chopped (optional)

Preheat the oven to 350°F. Line muffin tins with paper liners or spray with nonstick cooking spray.

In a mixing bowl, beat together the softened butter, softened cream cheese, sugar, and vanilla. Add eggs, one at a time, beating well after each addition. In a separate bowl, combine flour, baking powder, and salt, then gradually add to the butter mixture. Fold in berries and chopped nuts. Spoon batter into prepared muffin cups.

Bake for 25 to 30 minutes, or until tops are golden and a wooden toothpick inserted in the center of one of the muffins comes out clean. Cool on a wire rack for 15 minutes before removing from the tins.

Gathering the Garden

SOUPS, SALADS, AND VEGETABLE-FORWARD SIDES

CAULIFLOWER SOUP

Makes 6 to 8 servings

This is a very flavorful and filling soup. It is also very easy to make for a quick meal on a busy day. We especially love soups on cold winter days. Like the other soup recipes in this chapter, this pairs well with Sourdough Bread (p. 48).

4 cups chopped cauliflower

1 cup thinly sliced carrots

1 pound smoked sausage, cubed

½ cup chopped onion

⅓ cup all-purpose flour

¾ teaspoon salt

2 cups milk

8 ounces process cheese spread, cubed

Combine cauliflower and carrots with 2 cups water in a saucepan. Bring to a boil and cook until fork-tender. In a separate pot, brown sausage and onions. Add flour and salt to the meat mixture. Stir well. Gradually add the milk; bring to a boil. Cook and stir for 2 minutes. Add vegetables to cooking liquid; heat through. Stir in cheese spread until melted. Do not boil.

HAM AND BEAN SOUP

Makes 10 to 12 servings

We make bean soup with the fresh ham bones from pork butchering day. We freeze extra ham bones for later use as well.

1 pound dried Great Northern beans

1 meaty ham bone, or 2 smoked ham hocks

Salt, to taste

1 large onion, chopped

3 celery stalks, diced

2 carrots, peeled and shredded

½ teaspoon dried thyme

½ teaspoon pepper

1 can (28-ounce) crushed tomatoes in puree

2 tablespoons brown sugar

1½ cups finely shredded fresh spinach leaves

Sort and rinse beans. Place beans in a Dutch oven or soup pot; cover with water, and bring to a boil. Boil for 2 minutes. Remove from heat and let stand for 1 hour.

Drain beans and discard liquid, then return beans to the pot. Add ham bone or hocks, salt, and 3 quarts of water. Bring to a boil. Reduce heat and simmer, covered, for 1½ hours, or until meat easily falls from the bone. Remove bones from broth, trim off the meat, and discard the bones. Return meat to the pot and add onion, celery, carrots, salt, thyme, and pepper. Simmer, covered, for 1 hour, or until beans are tender. Add tomatoes and brown sugar. Cook for 10 minutes. Add spinach just before serving.

ASPARAGUS POTATO SOUP

Makes 4 to 6 servings

We have our own asparagus patch. We fix asparagus in a variety of ways, but this is our favorite. Crumbled crispy bacon works well as a garnish.

1¾ cups chicken broth

3 potatoes, peeled and cubed

⅓ cup chopped onion

1 teaspoon salt

½ pound asparagus, trimmed and cut into ½-inch pieces

1½ cups milk

2 tablespoons all-purpose flour

1 cup cubed process cheese spread or Colby cheese

Combine the broth, potatoes, onion, and salt in a large saucepan. Cook over medium heat until the vegetables are tender, about 20 minutes. Add the asparagus and cook for 10 minutes more.

Whisk the milk and flour together well in a small bowl, then whisk into the soup mixture. Stir in the cheese until melted. Pour into warmed soup bowls and serve immediately. If desired, garnish with crumbled bacon.

OVERNIGHT SALAD

Makes 24 servings

I make this frequently to take to potlucks because it can be made the night before. This salad was served at the wedding of daughter Loretta and son-in-law Dustin. Making it the day before meant one less job to do the day of the wedding. We stacked containers of salad in the cooler until ready to serve. For whipped salad dressing, I prefer to use Miracle Whip.

1 large head romaine or iceberg lettuce, chopped

1 head cauliflower, chopped

1 medium onion, chopped

3 carrots, peeled and chopped

1 pound fresh or frozen peas (no need to defrost)

1 cup whipped salad dressing

1 cup granulated sugar

1 cup shredded cheddar cheese

Salt and pepper, to taste

Mix the lettuce, cauliflower, onion, carrots, and peas together in a large bowl. In a separate bowl, combine the whipped salad dressing and sugar. Stir the dressing mixture until it is smooth and sugar is well incorporated. Pour the dressing over the vegetables and toss until they are evenly coated.

Sprinkle the cheese on top of the salad. Cover the bowl and chill the salad at least 8 hours or overnight in the refrigerator (works best stored in a 13 x 9-inch resealable plastic or glass container). Before serving, season to taste with salt and pepper.

COLESLAW

Makes 16 to 18 servings

I grow my own cabbage and carrots, so I make this recipe frequently at the end of gardening season. I always plant the Late Flat Dutch cabbage—it's ready later in the season and keeps well. For better flavor, I like adding a little ranch dressing to the coleslaw.

8 cups finely chopped cabbage
¼ cup grated carrots
⅓ cup granulated sugar
⅛ teaspoon onion powder
½ teaspoon salt
⅛ teaspoon ground pepper
½ cup mayonnaise
¼ cup buttermilk
¼ cup milk
2½ cups lemon juice
1½ tablespoons white vinegar
Paprika, to serve

Mix together cabbage and carrots in a large bowl.

In a separate small bowl, mix together sugar, onion powder, salt, and pepper. In another medium bowl, mix together mayonnaise, buttermilk, milk, lemon juice, and vinegar. Stir in the sugar mixture.

Add the mayonnaise mixture to the cabbage and carrots. Stir well to coat. Refrigerate for 3 to 5 hours.

Sprinkle with a light dusting of paprika before serving.

CORN CHIP SALAD

Makes 12 to 16 servings

This is sometimes served at weddings. The corn chips give the salad a nice crunch and a good flavor.

1 head iceberg or romaine lettuce, chopped
2 cups shredded cheddar cheese
1 pound bacon, fried and crumbled
6 hard-cooked eggs, peeled and chopped
2½ cups corn chips, crushed

Dressing
1 cup whipped salad dressing
¼ cup milk
2 tablespoons apple cider vinegar
¼ cup brown sugar
¼ cup granulated sugar

In a large bowl, toss together all salad ingredients except for corn chips. Whisk together dressing ingredients in a separate bowl. Just before serving, gently stir the dressing into the salad. Top with crushed corn chips.

TACO SALAD

Makes 16 to 18 servings

This was served at daughter Susan and Ervin's wedding. For this salad, the ground beef, onion and taco seasoning can be mixed beforehand. It is best to prepare the remaining ingredients shortly before serving. If using this dish for a potluck or carry-in item, keep the dressing and crushed chips in separate containers to mix in just before serving.

1 pound ground beef
1 cup chopped onion
1 (1-ounce) package taco seasoning
1 head lettuce, shredded
1 (8-ounce) package shredded cheddar cheese
1 cup diced fresh tomatoes
1 (15- or 16-ounce) can kidney beans, drained
2 cups (1 recipe) Thousand Island Dressing (p. 104)
1 (9.75-ounce) bag nacho cheese chips, crushed

In a large skillet, brown the ground beef with chopped onion and taco seasoning. Drain the grease from the ground beef mixture and set aside.

In a large bowl, mix together lettuce, shredded cheese, tomatoes, and beans.

Just before serving, add the ground beef mixture to the lettuce mixture and combine well. Stir in the dressing, then top with crushed chips.

LOADED PASTA SALAD

Makes 20 to 24 servings

This is a new salad that I started making recently, and it is fast becoming a favorite. The sweet corn gives it an unexpected flavor. We love the variation of cubed cheese instead of shredded in this salad. I typically use Sweet Baby Ray's barbecue sauce.

1 pound rotini pasta	**1 cup mayonnaise**
1 tablespoon olive oil	**¼ cup barbecue sauce**
1 pound thick-cut bacon, chopped	**1 tablespoon Worcestershire sauce**
½ pound lean ground beef	**2 tablespoons spicy mustard**
½ teaspoon garlic powder	**1 (15-ounce) can sweet corn, drained**
½ teaspoon onion powder	**2 cups fresh tomatoes, diced**
⅛ teaspoon crushed red pepper flakes	**¾ cup diced green onions**
Salt and pepper, to taste	**1½ cups cubed Colby cheese**

Cook rotini pasta according to package instructions; drain pasta and rinse with cold water. Drizzle pasta with 1 tablespoon olive oil and set aside.

In a large skillet over medium heat, cook bacon until crispy. Remove bacon to a paper towel–lined plate, leaving a little bit of bacon grease in the pan. Add ground beef to the skillet and cook until browned. Season cooked ground beef with garlic powder, onion powder, crushed red pepper flakes, and salt and pepper.

Skim away the remaining grease and remove the pan from heat.

In a large serving bowl, combine mayonnaise, barbecue sauce, Worcestershire sauce, and spicy mustard, and whisk until smooth.

Add cooked pasta, bacon, ground beef, corn, tomatoes, green onions, and Colby cheese, and toss until fully combined. Refrigerate until ready to serve.

KEEPING UP WITH THE GARDEN

*K*eeping up with the garden needs is never-ending through the spring and summertime. My sister Susan and I loved to weed the garden together as girls. Susan would tell me all kinds of interesting stories and time went so much faster that way. The only thing that would slow us down is when we found some scary bug. The whole family often went out and worked in the garden on Saturdays. Working together made it more enjoyable, and I will always treasure those memories.

—*Daughter Verena*

Planting a garden requires a little brain work and planning to prepare and figure out where to plant everything. We never like to plant the same thing in the same area as we did the year before. For example, we plant sweet corn at one end and potatoes at the other end and then the next year we rotate the layout. We need to make sure we don't plant hot peppers beside green bell peppers, or the green peppers will be hot! Watermelon and cucumbers must also be planted separately. In one of our first gardens, Joe and I planted watermelon and cucumbers beside each other, and the cucumbers grew short and fat. Some things we learn from general knowledge and some things from experience. After thirty years of gardening, we have grown wiser with time. Live and learn proves true—we grow most from our mistakes.

We usually have a good farm dog around that keeps deer, raccoons, and other pests out of the gardens. We used to have a few rat terrier dogs that kept the moles under control in the garden and yard. Now the weeds are a different story! I dislike weeding, but it has to be done. We've made the process much simpler by building some raised garden beds. It's easier to reach the weeds, and there are fewer of them.

The garden's bounty makes meal planning so straightforward in the summer months. A meal can be assembled very quickly from zucchini, sweet corn, tomatoes, cucumbers, fresh red potatoes, and green beans. The yummy sweet corn is always a treat. And nothing is better than the taste of that first radish, lettuce, or tomato. The first small bowl of radishes has to be shared by all of us; it makes your mouth water for more.

—*Lovina*

CARROT AND CELERY BAKE

Makes 6 servings

I like to make this flavorful baked dish when I have lots of carrots and celery on hand that need to be used up. Our children prefer it without the almonds, but my husband, Joe, loves dishes with almost any kind of nuts.

3 cups chopped carrots (½-inch pieces)

3 cups sliced celery (½-inch pieces)

**1½ cups shredded process cheese spread
   (may substitute Colby or cheddar cheese)**

1 (10½-ounce) can cream of chicken soup, not diluted

⅓ cup slivered or sliced almonds

1 tablespoon butter

Cook carrots and celery in a pot of boiling water for 8 minutes; drain. Alternate layers of celery, carrots, shredded cheese spread, and dollops of soup in a greased 6-quart baking dish, ending with a layer of soup. In a small frying pan, lightly toast the almonds in the butter. Sprinkle them over the top soup layer. Bake at 350°F for 20 to 30 minutes, or until the dish is hot and bubbling all the way through.

SPINACH CASSEROLE

Makes 8 servings

I love spinach now, but as a child I did not care for it. This casserole is an especially flavorful preparation of cooked spinach. Fresh spinach works well in a salad instead of or in addition to lettuce.

16 ounces fresh or frozen spinach, thawed and squeezed dry if frozen
¾ pound cheese, grated
2 cups cooked rice
4 eggs, beaten
¾ cup milk
¼ cup (½ stick) butter, melted
1 tablespoon Worcestershire sauce
1 tablespoon onion flakes
1 tablespoon salt

In a large bowl, combine the spinach, cheese, and cooked rice. In a medium bowl, whisk together the eggs, milk, melted butter, Worcestershire sauce, onion flakes, and salt. Pour the egg mixture over the spinach mixture and stir well to combine. Spread the mixture evenly in a greased 4-quart baking dish. Bake at 350°F for 45 to 50 minutes.

VEGETABLE MEAT LOAF

Makes 6 to 8 servings

This meat loaf includes a lot of vegetables, which makes it an excellent all-in-one meal. It tastes like a cross between meat loaf and dressing (also known as stuffing).

1½ pounds ground beef

1 onion, finely chopped

1 cup chopped cabbage

1 cup peeled and diced red potatoes

1 cup diced carrots

1 cup bread crumbs

1 cup milk

1 egg, beaten

1 tablespoon butter, melted

1 teaspoon salt

¼ teaspoon pepper

Glaze (optional)

½ cup brown sugar

2 teaspoons yellow mustard

1 tablespoon Worcestershire sauce

1 tablespoon apple cider vinegar

In a large skillet, brown the ground beef. Drain the grease. In a large bowl, mix together the beef, onion, cabbage, potatoes, carrots, and bread crumbs. Whisk together the milk, egg, butter, salt, and pepper, and pour over the beef mixture. Stir well. Press into a 9 x 5-inch loaf pan. If opting to add glaze, mix all glaze ingredients together in a small bowl and pour over loaf before baking. Bake at 350°F for 1 hour until vegetables are cooked through and top is browned.

CHEESY MASHED POTATOES

Makes 8 servings

This is nice to have with an evening meal and can be doubled or tripled for a crowd. It works well as a carry-in dish for potlucks or sharing with others. It also tastes delicious topped with gravy or chili.

6 large potatoes, peeled

⅓ cup chopped onion

1 (8-ounce) package cream cheese

1 cup shredded cheese, plus additional for serving (any cheese works, but we prefer Colby or Colby Jack)

½ cup sour cream

1 egg, beaten

2 teaspoons salt

½ teaspoon pepper

Place the potatoes in a medium saucepan and cover with water. Bring potatoes to a boil and cook until soft. Drain water and mash the potatoes in the pot. Add remaining ingredients to potatoes and beat until fluffy. Put mashed potatoes in a greased 13 x 9-inch baking dish. Bake, covered, at 350°F until heated through, or 20 to 25 minutes. Sprinkle with additional cheese if desired.

CAMPFIRE POTATOES

Makes 4 servings

We use red potatoes from our garden for this recipe. Campfire Potatoes are fun and easy to make on the grill on a hot summer day when it's too warm to cook in the house. We generally use a charcoal grill, but one year I received a gas grill for my birthday from my husband Joe. I use the gas grill when I do the grilling because it sits on my front porch and is easy to access to check the food.

5 medium potatoes, peeled and sliced
¼ cup grated Parmesan cheese
2 teaspoons minced fresh parsley
¾ teaspoon garlic powder
½ teaspoon salt
⅛ teaspoon pepper
¼ cup (½ stick) butter

Place half the potatoes on a large piece of foil (the foil should be big enough to fold and seal over the top of the potatoes). Sprinkle the potatoes evenly with Parmesan cheese, parsley, garlic powder, salt, and pepper. Dot with butter. Top with remaining potatoes. Fold foil over; seal tightly. Grill, covered, over medium heat for 30 to 35 minutes, or until potatoes are tender.

GREEN FRIED TOMATOES

Makes 4 to 6 servings

We pick all the remaining green tomatoes from the plants before the first frost in the fall. This recipe is an effective and delicious way to use them up at the end of gardening season.

2 eggs
½ cup milk
1 cup all-purpose flour
Salt and pepper, as desired
4 green tomatoes, sliced ½ inch thick
Shortening, for frying (enough for 1 to 1½ inches depth in the skillet)

Whisk together eggs and milk in a small bowl. In a separate bowl, whisk together flour and salt and pepper. Dip sliced tomatoes in egg mixture. Then dip tomato slices in seasoned flour to coat. Put prepared slices on a plate. Heat shortening in a skillet over medium-high heat and fry tomatoes until brown on both sides. Drain on a paper towel–lined plate. Enjoy!

ONION RINGS

Makes 2 to 4 servings

Each year we plant a lot of sweet onions—sometimes as many as two hundred! We love to pick and eat some like we would green onions while they're still small. Once the other onions are big, we prefer to slice them for sandwiches or to make these onion rings.

¼ cup milk
1 egg, beaten lightly
2 tablespoons canola or vegetable oil
½ cup all-purpose flour
½ teaspoon baking powder
¼ teaspoons salt
Oil or lard, for frying
1 large onion, sliced into rings about ½ inch thick

Mix together milk, egg, oil, flour, baking powder, and salt in a pie plate or shallow baking dish. Pour oil into a small heavy-bottomed pot to a depth of about 2 inches. Heat oil over medium heat until a deep-fry thermometer reads 375°F. Dip onion rings in egg mixture and fry in hot oil on each side until golden brown, about 2 minutes per side. Drain on a paper towel–lined plate.

Putting Food By

SAUCES, SPREADS, PICKLES, AND PRESERVES

MILD HOT PEPPER BUTTER

Makes about 6 pints

We love this spread on sandwiches or on toast for breakfast. It is also good on tacos or Haystack Dinners (p. 216). It can be used almost like a salsa. This recipe makes a batch for canning, but you could prepare a half or quarter recipe if you prefer to make it for eating fresh. It will store in the refrigerator for several weeks.

12 jalapeño peppers
16 ounces (2 cups) prepared yellow mustard
6 cups granulated sugar
4 cups white vinegar
1 tablespoon salt
1½ cups all-purpose flour
1½ cups water

Prepare 6 pint jars, lids, and bands for canning according to manufacturer's instructions.

Remove stems, membranes, and seeds from jalapeño peppers and chop the peppers finely; you may want to wear gloves and use a handheld chopper or food processor. In a large saucepan, mix chopped peppers with mustard, sugar, vinegar, and salt. Bring to a boil and boil for 10 to 15 minutes. Stir together flour and water in a medium bowl, then slowly add to pepper mixture. Boil 5 minutes more. Stir often to keep from sticking. Pour thickened pepper butter into prepared pint jars. Wipe rims, cover with lids and bands, and process and seal in a boiling water canner for 15 minutes according to canning jar and lid manufacturer's instructions.

Note: Canning times are subject to change according to USDA regulations. Check your county extension office.

SALSA

Makes about 6 pints

We usually increase the amount of hot peppers listed here because we like our salsa spicy. This salsa can be used on my recipe for Haystack Dinner (p. 216) as well as on tacos, scrambled eggs, breakfast burritos, skillets, casseroles, and so on. We also serve this as a snack with tortilla chips at potlucks or family gatherings.

10 tomatoes, peeled and chopped

3 cups chopped onion

2 green bell peppers, chopped

4 jalapeño peppers, chopped

1 (12-ounce) can tomato paste

½ cup white vinegar

1 tablespoon garlic powder

1 tablespoon salt

Combine all the ingredients in a large saucepan. Bring the mixture to a boil and simmer for 2 hours. Allow to cool and serve with your favorite chips. Leftover salsa can be frozen in quart-sized freezer bags for up to 3 months.

PIZZA SAUCE

Makes about 30 pints

We like to make this pizza sauce to use in pizza casseroles and on pizza. It can also work as a pasta sauce. A Victorio strainer separates fruit and vegetable puree from skins, and seeds. A food mill can also work. Clear Jel is a modified corn-starch designed for thickening. It is often available in bulk food stores.

This recipe makes a large amount, but if you have limited freezer space or fewer people in your household, you may wish to make a half or quarter recipe.

3 gallons tomatoes, roughly chopped
4 onions, roughly chopped
4 cloves garlic, peeled
½ cup minced fresh parsley
1 cup granulated sugar
½ cup salt
1 tablespoon paprika
1 tablespoon chili powder
2 tablespoons dried oregano
1½ cups Clear Jel
1 quart cold water

In a large pot, cook tomatoes, onions, garlic, and parsley until soft enough to put through a Victorio strainer. Put strained juice in another large pot (a 3-gallon pot works best) and add sugar, salt, paprika, chili powder, and oregano. Bring to a boil.

Mix together Clear Jel and cold water, then add Clear Jel mixture to the tomato mixture, stirring constantly. Boil for 10 minutes, then remove from heat. When sauce has cooled, pour into prepared pint jars or quart-sized re-sealable plastic bags and store in the freezer for up to 6 months.

PIZZA DIP

Makes 12 servings

This tasty dip goes well with chips and crackers and is the perfect snack to take to a family gathering. If you love pizza, you most likely will love this dip. My recipe for Pizza Sauce (p. 97) works well for this dish.

1 (8-ounce) package cream cheese, softened
½ cup sour cream
1 teaspoon dried oregano
¼ teaspoon garlic powder
⅛ tablespoon crushed red pepper
½ cup pizza sauce
½ cup pepperoni, chopped
½ cup chopped onion
½ cup chopped green bell pepper
½ cup shredded mozzarella cheese

Mix together cream cheese, sour cream, pepperoni, oregano, garlic powder, and crushed red pepper. Spread into the bottom of a greased 9-inch square baking pan and top with pizza sauce, followed by onions and bell peppers.

Bake at 350°F for 12 minutes. Remove from the oven and sprinkle with mozzarella cheese. Return to the oven until the cheese is melted. Serve with tortilla chips or crackers.

PRESERVING THE GARDEN

We grow a variety of vegetables and fruits both for fresh eating and putting by. We preserve green beans, corn, salsa, tomato juice, V8 juice, pizza and spaghetti sauces, red beets, pickles, cabbage, hot peppers, jams, jellies, and rhubarb juice. Then we have strawberries, grape juice, applesauce, peaches, pears, and other fruits for pie fillings that we get from the local U-pick fruit farm. Sometimes a neighbor, friend, or a church family has extra fruit from their trees to share with us. We had peach and apple trees in the early years of our marriage, but sadly they had to be cut down for our new house almost eighteen years ago, and we never did plant more.

We used to plant a hundred or more tomato plants every year, but with our children growing older and getting married and having homes of their own, we have downsized a lot. This year we ended up planting sixty plants. On a good yield that would be a lot, but the crop wasn't as plentiful, so the amount was just right. If I have excess in garden crops, I share with family or friends.

I usually let my plants in the garden produce up until the first frost in the fall. Some people pull them out when they have enough tomatoes and want to clear up the garden before colder weather sets in. I like to get as much yield as I can from the plants. In October we will still have tomatoes, green peppers, hot peppers, carrots, and late cabbage growing in the garden (and watermelon, if I planted any). Usually those are the last crops of the year.

Canning season was always busy, and the children learned to help at a young age. We would harvest as many vegetables as we could from our garden, filling hundreds of jars to put on the shelves in the canning room in the basement. Onions were hung to dry and potatoes stored in the cool canning room. Some years we had enough onions and potatoes to hold us until the next spring. Other years the crop wasn't so good.

I enjoy canning if there is plenty of time. If you are short on time, it can become overwhelming. I remember that as a young mother with small children, the task always looked harder. Daughter Susan had ten bushels of apples to make into applesauce this year. She had help from her mother-in-law, sisters-in-law, sisters, aunt, and mother, so the job was done in one day. What a relief for a mother of five young children!

Though canning makes for long, tiresome days, it is always helpful to have preserved food on hand. I feel refreshed seeing the fruits of my family's labor lined up on the shelves in the canning room in the basement.

—Lovina

SWEET DILL PICKLES

Makes 3 quarts

I usually serve these pickles when we host church services. I grow my own dill and use Palace King cucumbers for this recipe; they stay very crisp when canned. Though they have a rougher skin, when peeled they also work well for eating fresh.

Pickling cucumbers, sliced (enough to fill three 1-quart jars)
12 garlic cloves, divided (4 per quart)
6 heads dill, or 3 teaspoon dill seeds, divided (2 heads, or 1 teaspoon, per quart)
3 pinches alum powder, divided (1 per quart)
2 cups white vinegar
2 cups water
3 cups granulated sugar
2 tablespoons canning and pickling salt

Prepare 3 quart jars, lids, and bands for canning according to manufacturer's instructions.

Divide sliced cucumbers, garlic, dill, and alum into prepared quart jars. In a large stock pot, heat vinegar, water, sugar, and salt until the sugar and salt are dissolved. Pour hot liquid over the cucumbers, leaving ½-inch headspace above the brine. Wipe rims of jars, cover with lids and bands, and process in a boiling water canner for 15 minutes according to the manufacturer's instructions.

Note: Canning times are subject to change according to USDA regulations. Check your county extension office.

THOUSAND ISLAND DRESSING

Makes about 2 cups dressing

This goes well on many salads, including Taco Salad (p. 77). When daughter Susan was married to Ervin, they served taco salad with Thousand Island dressing.

1 cup whipped salad dressing
½ cup granulated sugar
¼ cup ketchup
¼ cup pickle relish
¼ teaspoon salt
Dash pepper

Combine all ingredients in a bowl and stir till well blended. Store in a covered glass container in the refrigerator for up to 1 month.

CHICKEN GRAVY

Makes 6 cups

This is a quick and easy gravy. We like to serve it over mashed potatoes or dressing (also known as stuffing). When we raise chickens for meat, the chicken broth we make from the cooked chicken goes fast, as we use it often to prepare dishes for weddings, church meals, and other gatherings.

4½ cups chicken broth
1½ tablespoons chicken soup base
Pinch garlic salt
2½ tablespoons cornstarch
2 tablespoons all-purpose flour
½ cup milk, divided
1 large egg, slightly beaten

Combine the broth, soup base, and garlic salt in a medium saucepan. Bring to a boil. Mix together the cornstarch, flour, and ¼ cup milk in a small bowl, then stir into the broth mixture. Whisk together the egg and remaining ¼ cup of milk. Gradually whisk egg mixture into hot broth, and continue whisking until the gravy is thickened.

SPICY CHICKEN DIP

Makes 6 to 8 cups

This is a zesty dip for people who love spicy food. If you don't prefer spice, you can use another kind of cheese and omit the chili powder.

4 cups thick tomato sauce
½ cup chopped celery
1½ cups diced red bell pepper
1 onion, diced
1 teaspoon chili powder
1 teaspoon garlic powder
½ teaspoon ground celery seed
Pepper, to taste
Seasoned salt, to taste
3 tablespoons all-purpose flour
2 cups fully cooked and diced chicken breast (bite-sized pieces)
1½ cups cubed pepper jack cheese (¼-inch cubes)
Tortilla chips, for serving

In a large saucepan, combine tomato sauce, celery, pepper, onion, chili powder, garlic pepper, ground celery seed, pepper, and seasoned salt. Simmer 30 minutes. In a small bowl, mix the flour with 3 tablespoons water. Add the flour mixture to the pan and stir to make the tomato sauce creamy. Add chicken breast pieces and stir to combine. Place mixture in a shallow 13 x 9-inch baking dish. Keep hot in a warm (200°F) oven. Just before serving, top with pepper jack cheese cubes. Serve with tortilla chips for dipping, and shredded lettuce, sour cream, or any other toppings you prefer.

STRAWBERRY BUTTER

Makes about 2 cups

This is sometimes served at spring weddings when strawberries are in season. The combination replaces strawberry jam and butter. It goes especially well with Mystery Biscuits (p. 50).

6 large fresh strawberries, hulled and at room temperature
1 cup (2 sticks) butter, softened to room temperature
¾ cup powdered sugar

Chop strawberries and put into a medium bowl, then add butter and powdered sugar and blend well with a whisk, pastry blender, or hand mixer. If needed, add more powdered sugar to taste to reach a spreading consistency that is at your desired sweetness.

CINNAMON BUTTER

Makes about 2 cups

Like Strawberry Butter, this sweet spread is also served at weddings instead of plain butter. It's perfect to top Oatmeal Pancakes (p. 35) or biscuits made using Quick Baking Mix (p. 55).

1 cup (2 sticks) butter, softened to room temperature
1 cup powdered sugar
1 cup honey
2 teaspoons ground cinnamon

In a large bowl, whip the butter until it's nice and creamy. Mix in the powdered sugar. Then add the honey and the cinnamon. Whip the mixture well. Scrape the sides of the bowl and whip it a little more to make sure the ingredients are thoroughly combined.

DECORATOR'S CREAM CHEESE FROSTING

Makes about 4 cups

This can be used for icing a cake, or cinnamon rolls, cookies, or whatever treat you prefer. It works well on Speedy Cinnamon Rolls (p. 58) and Spice Cake (p. 176).

½ cup shortening
½ cup (1 stick) butter, softened to room temperature
1 (8-ounce) package cream cheese, softened to room temperature
1 tablespoon vanilla extract
8 cups powdered sugar

Cream together the shortening, butter, and cream cheese in a large bowl. Blend in the vanilla. Gradually add in all the powdered sugar and keep mixing until you reach your desired consistency. The frosting can be thinned with a little milk if needed.

HOMEMADE FRUIT PIE FILLING

Makes 6 quarts

I enjoy making my own fruit pie filling. You can use it in so many ways, such as in puddings, pies, cakes, and more. See Danish Breakfast Bars (p. 40), Fruit-Filled Oatmeal Squares (p. 206), Cake Delight (p. 233), and Cherry Bars for a Crowd (p. 237).

6 cups granulated sugar

2¼ cups instant Clear Jel

7 cups cold water

½ cup fresh lemon juice

6 quarts fresh fruit, such as cherries (pitted), blueberries, raspberries, or peaches (pitted and sliced)

In a large stock pot, combine the sugar and instant Clear Jel over medium-high heat. Add the water and stir well. Cook on medium-high until the mixture thickens and begins to bubble, about 7 minutes. Add the lemon juice and boil for 1 minute, stirring constantly. Fold in the fruit, then remove from the heat. If not used immediately, divide the cooled pie filling into quart-sized resealable plastic bags and freeze for up to 4 to 6 months.

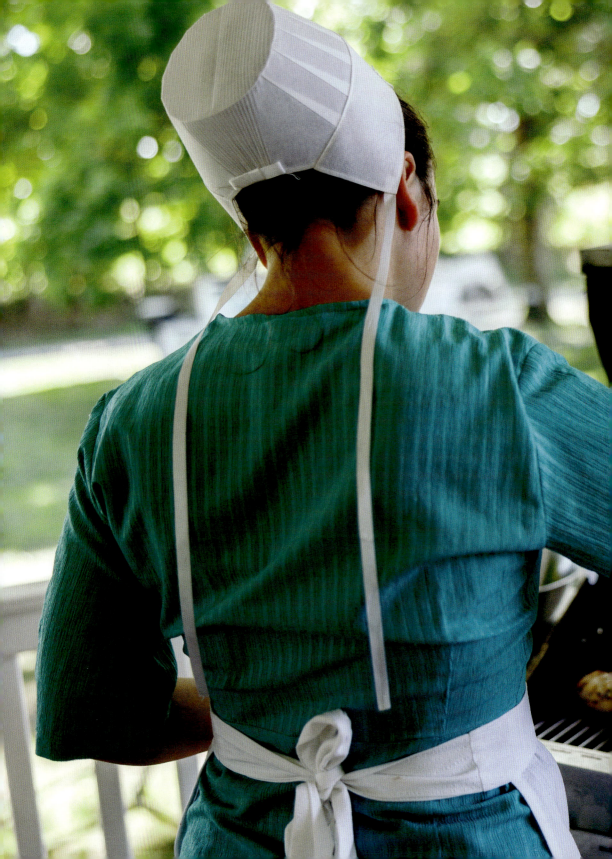

Harvesting Field and Forest

MEAT, POULTRY, FISH, AND GAME

HERB ROASTED CHICKEN

Makes 4 to 5 servings

I do not care much for sweet potatoes by themselves, but I can enjoy them when they are fixed with chicken and a few other ingredients. The potatoes give the chicken a unique flavor.

1 pound chicken thighs (either bone-in or boneless)
1 onion, diced
1 sweet potato, peeled and roughly chopped
3 red potatoes, roughly chopped

Sauce
½ cup (1 stick) butter, melted
4 cloves garlic, crushed
1 tablespoon fresh minced parsley
1 teaspoon brown sugar
½ teaspoon poultry seasoning
½ teaspoon cayenne pepper
½ teaspoon salt
½ teaspoon pepper

Arrange chicken thighs and distribute the onion, sweet potato, and red potatoes evenly in a 13 x 9-inch baking pan.

Combine all sauce ingredients and blend together in a small bowl. Pour sauce over chicken and vegetables. Bake, covered, at 350°F for 45 minutes, then uncover and bake for an additional 45 minutes.

BARBECUE RANCH CHICKEN SALAD

Makes 4 to 6 servings

Butchering chickens for meat involves hard work, but the entire family pitches in to help out. It is very handy to have a supply of your own homegrown chicken in the freezer.

10 to 12 cups torn lettuce

2 cups grilled and sliced chicken

1 cup whole kernel corn

1 cup black beans, rinsed and drained

A few ⅛-inch thick slices red or sweet onion

1 cup shredded cheddar cheese, divided

1½ cups ranch salad dressing

½ cup barbecue sauce

2 soft tortilla shells, cut into strips

In a larger bowl, toss lettuce with grilled chicken slices, corn, black beans, onions, and most of the shredded cheese. Reserve some cheese for the top.

Pour the ranch salad dressing and barbecue sauce over salad. Gently combine.

Top salad with remaining cheese and tortilla strips. Serve immediately.

RANCH PARMESAN CHICKEN

Makes 4 to 6 servings

Our family enjoys eating chicken fixed many different ways. On a busy day this is an easy and tasty way to prepare chicken. Our children love ranch dressing on a lot of different foods! For the ingredients that offer a range in measurement, choose an amount based on your preference.

1 cup dry breadcrumbs
¼ to ⅓ cup Parmesan cheese
1 teaspoon seasoned salt
½ to 1 teaspoon ground black pepper
½ to 1 teaspoon garlic powder
6 boneless, skinless chicken breasts
1 cup prepared ranch salad dressing (bottled dressing can be used as well)
¼ cup (½ stick) butter, melted

Set oven rack to lowest position and preheat the oven to 400°F. Lightly grease a 13 x 9-inch baking pan. (For easier cleanup, line the pan with nonstick aluminum foil or parchment paper instead. Do not use a smaller baking dish, or the bottom of the chicken will be soggy.)

In a shallow bowl, mix together the dry breadcrumbs with Parmesan cheese, seasoned salt, black pepper, and garlic powder. Pour the salad dressing in another bowl. Dip the chicken in the salad dressing to coat both sides; allow any excess to drip off. Coat each chicken breast in the breadcrumb mixture. Place coated chicken in the prepared baking pan in a single layer. Lightly drizzle melted butter over each piece. Bake, uncovered, for 30 to 35 minutes, or until the chicken is cooked through.

TURKEY BURGERS

Makes 10 patties

This is a wonderful way to use up leftover turkey after a Thanksgiving feast—we finely chop the cooked meat in place of ground turkey. Our children love it when I mix some ranch dressing into the mixture before cooking. When I do so, I usually add about ½ cup dressing to the mixture.

1 pound ground turkey

2 cups cooked rice

¼ cup chopped onion

¼ cup ketchup

1 egg, beaten

1 tablespoon Worcestershire sauce

1½ teaspoons salt

1 teaspoon black pepper

⅛ teaspoon garlic powder

Combine the ingredients, mixing well. Shape into 10 even patties. Cook over medium-high heat in a hot skillet coated with cooking spray for 10 to 12 minutes on each side.

BUSY BUTCHERING DAYS

I always love pork butchering day. The whole family gets together to help out. A few of the women will make the lunch, which consists of mashed potatoes, gravy, corn, pork tenderloin, and lots of other food. The rest of us help cut up meat and grind meat for sausage. We throw all the bones in a big kettle over a fire. The men take turns stirring it with a long fork. This will be used for ponhoss, also known as scrapple, which is often served at breakfast. The lard is also rendered, and we get to enjoy the cracklings. We add some seasoning and everyone snacks on them.

I always think it's fun getting together, talking with others while cutting up meat, standing outside by the kettle, and watching the process unfold. It's usually pretty chilly outside, so we try to stay warm by the kettle while snacking on cracklings and listening to the men share their hunting stories. The older, more experienced butchers usually show the younger ones what to do, where to cut, and so on. This way we learn a lot of things, and someday we'll teach the younger ones. It's great to have the independence of being able to raise, can, and freeze your own food.

—Daughter Lovina

Pork butchering day is always a long day, and it is good to have plenty of help. It is also an enjoyable day to spend with family. Many hands make lighter work! First the pigs are dressed, and then two big black kettles are set up to start heating water to cook the meat off the bones. The hams, tenderloins, bacon, and ribs are separated, and the rest of the meat is cut out for sausage. The fat gets cut into one-inch cubes for rendering. We also save the liver, brains, heart, and tongue.

The lard is rendered in one kettle, and the bones are cooked in the other. When the meat starts to come off the bones, it is brought inside and the meat is picked off the bones. It is then put through a grinder. Liver pudding can be made from this meat, and we always put it all in our ponhoss, as we think that the more meat in the ponhoss, the better the taste. To make the ponhoss, the broth from the bones is strained, measured, and poured back into the kettle. Then the meat and seasonings are added. We usually add two tablespoons of salt and one tablespoon of black pepper to a gallon of broth. When the broth is at a hard boil, we gradually sift in flour. Someone needs to stir the mixture constantly. The men and boys take turns stirring; with twelve to fifteen gallons of broth, it gets harder to stir when the flour is added. This takes some muscles! We add four cups of flour to each gallon of broth. Some people use cornmeal instead of flour to thicken the ponhoss, but I prefer flour. When the mixture is at a rolling boil and the men agree that it is ready to take off the fire, then the fire is put out. The ponhoss is dipped from the kettle into big, galvanized metal tubs. While it is still hot, we fill 13 x 9-inch foil pans with the ponhoss (or cake pans can be used). The ponhoss is then set in a cool place to chill. Once the mixture is set it can be sliced and fried.

The sausage is ground, packaged, and put in the freezer. I always like to can some as well to put in a casserole or soup or to make breakfast sausage gravy for a quicker meal. The *fischlie*, or backstrap, is a small tenderloin just under the spine at the rear end of the pig's body cavity. For as long as I can remember, this was fried for lunch on butchering day, and served with a full menu of mashed potatoes, gravy, dressing, a vegetable dish, salad, and so on. The men were always hungry for a good meal on a hard work day.

Later in the day, the hams, tenderloins, and ribs are sliced and packaged for the freezer. Years ago we didn't have a freezer, so a lot of this had to be canned or eaten fresh. The bacon is set in a tub of marinade to season it before it is sliced and frozen. The cracklings are munched on throughout the day after the lard is put through the lard press. The lard is poured into glass jars while it's still very hot and lids are put on. Lard seals and stores very nicely like this for the next year's supply. Then comes the cleanup, a greasy job that requires a lot of hot water and soap.

We have also raised beef cows and chickens for meat, and those butchering days are full-day ordeals as well. When the children were all at home, the whole family would help, from the youngest to the oldest. A few were designated as the "chicken catchers" to round up the birds. Joe would take care of the chicken's heads, and then a few other children helped pluck feathers. I would do the gutting, and a few would help clean the birds. Then I cut up the meat. Sometimes we would put the whole chickens on ice, and Joe would help me cut them up later. It was an interesting and unusual day, but we were always glad to be done.

—Lovina

PORK CHOP CASSEROLE

Makes 4 servings

This is a very tasty way to fix pork chops. It's also an easy way to supply a protein and vegetables all in one dish. Other vegetables can be added, if desired. I always put in more onions than the recipe calls for. To season the pork chops, I use a mixture of salt, ground black pepper, lemon pepper, seasoned salt, and garlic salt.

4 pork chops, seasoned as desired

4 cups sliced red potatoes

1 cup diced celery

1 cup diced carrots

1 (10½-ounce) can cream of mushroom soup

1 cup milk

2 tablespoons chopped onion

½ teaspoon salt

1 teaspoon pepper

1 cup grated American cheese

In a large nonstick skillet, sear seasoned pork chops until they are golden brown on both sides. Place potatoes, celery, and carrots in a greased 13 x 9-inch baking dish. Mix together soup, milk, onion, salt, and pepper in a medium bowl. Pour soup mixture over the vegetables and potatoes. Place seared pork chops over the vegetables and potatoes.

Bake, uncovered, at 375°F for about 1 hour, or until potatoes are tender. A few minutes before the dish is finished baking, sprinkle with the cheese and allow it to melt.

BARBECUED PORK RIBS

Makes 4 to 6 servings

We butcher our own pork, so we usually have our own ribs on hand to barbecue. Sometimes we grill them, but on cold winter days, this is a great way to make ribs inside.

1 cup apple cider vinegar

¾ cup ketchup

¼ cup granulated sugar

1 teaspoon paprika

1 teaspoon chili powder

3 tablespoons canola or vegetable oil

6 country-style ribs

3 tablespoons all-purpose flour

In a medium bowl, make a liquid mixture with the vinegar, ketchup, sugar, paprika, and chili powder. Let stand for 30 minutes. Pour oil in a frying pan and turn the pan to medium heat, allowing it to heat for a few minutes. While the pan is heating, put the flour in a shallow dish, then roll ribs in the flour. Fry ribs in the hot oil until browned. Place the browned ribs in a 6-quart baking dish and pour the liquid mixture over the ribs. Bake at 350°F for 1 hour, depending on the size of the ribs. (Pork should reach an internal temperature of 145°F after a 3-minute rest time before consuming.) Cover baking dish during baking for more moist ribs.

YUMMASETTI

Makes 12 servings

I made this casserole a lot when the children were younger. I often used frozen mixed vegetables instead of peas; you can substitute the same amount, if desired. This creamy meat and pasta casserole is a winner in our household.

3 pounds ground beef

1 medium onion, chopped

1 (16-ounce) package egg noodles, or 1 pound homemade noodles

2 cups fresh or frozen peas

2 (10¾-ounce) cans cream of mushroom soup

1 (10¾-ounce) can cream of chicken soup

1 cup sour cream

10 slices white or wheat bread, toasted and cubed

2 cups shredded cheese (any kind)

Preheat the oven to 350°F. Grease a 6-quart baking dish and set aside.

In a large skillet, cook the ground beef and onion over medium heat. Remove from heat when the beef is browned. Drain the grease and transfer the meat mixture to a large bowl.

Cook the egg noodles in salted boiling water according to the package directions until tender. Drain well.

Add the cooked noodles, peas, mushroom soup, chicken soup, sour cream, and toasted bread cubes to the meat mixture. Stir until all the ingredients are well combined. Transfer the mixture to the prepared baking dish and top with shredded cheese. Bake, uncovered, for about 30 minutes, or until the casserole is bubbling and the cheese is melted.

ZUCCHINI BEEF CASSEROLE

Makes 4 to 6 servings

We make this casserole frequently when we have an abundance of zucchini. This calls for a cup of the Quick Baking Mix (p. 55), which works well as a substitute for store-bought mixes like Bisquick.

1 pound ground beef
1 (1¼-ounce) package taco seasoning
4 large eggs
½ cup olive oil
1 teaspoon fresh minced parsley (optional)
½ teaspoon salt
½ teaspoon black pepper
3 cups shredded zucchini
¼ cup shredded onion
1 cup Quick Baking Mix (p. 55)
½ cup shredded cheese (any kind)

Preheat the oven to 350°F. Grease a 13 x 9-inch baking dish.

Brown the ground beef in a large skillet and stir in the taco seasoning. Drain and set aside.

Beat the eggs, oil, parsley (if using), salt, and pepper together in a large bowl until blended. Stir in the shredded zucchini, shredded onion, and baking mix, mixing well. Stir in the cooked ground beef until distributed evenly in the mixture. Pour into the prepared baking dish and spread out evenly.

Bake for 30 minutes, then sprinkle cheese evenly over top. Continue baking until the cheese is melted, about 10 minutes. Remove from the oven and spoon onto individual plates to serve.

STEAK CHILI

Makes 12 servings

My usual chili recipe calls for sausage instead of steak and there are a few other differences, but this steak version doesn't last long around here whenever I make a pot of it. It is very delicious! I make it more often around beef butchering time when I have fresh beef.

2 tablespoons vegetable oil, divided

2 cups chopped onion

4 cloves garlic, minced

1 large red pepper, diced

1 cup chopped celery

1 pound sirloin steak, cut into ½-inch cubes

2 tablespoons chili powder

1 teaspoon cumin

½ teaspoon dried oregano

2 (19-ounce) cans red kidney beans, drained

1 (28-ounce) can stewed tomatoes, with juice

1 (5½-ounce) can tomato paste

1 tablespoon lemon juice

2 teaspoons Worcestershire sauce

½ teaspoon hot sauce

Salt and pepper, to taste

In a large saucepan or Dutch oven, heat 1 tablespoon oil and cook the onion and garlic over medium heat for 5 minutes. Add red pepper and celery and cook for another 5 minutes until softened. Remove vegetables from the pan and place in a bowl. Add the remaining 1 tablespoon oil and brown the steak cubes in batches (do not crowd the pan). Add the browned steak to the bowl of vegetables. When all the steak has been browned, return the vegetables and steak to the pan, over low heat. Add the chili powder, cumin, and oregano. Cook and stir for 1 minute. Add the kidney beans, tomatoes, and tomato paste. Bring to a boil, then reduce heat, cover, and simmer for about 45 minutes until meat is tender. Stir in lemon juice, Worcestershire sauce, hot sauce, and salt and pepper. Remove from heat and serve.

BARBECUE BEEF SANDWICHES

Makes 10 to 12 servings

This recipe is similar to pulled pork sandwiches, except it's made with beef. We like beef fixed almost any way—fried, baked, grilled, deep-fried, and so on!

3 pounds beef bottom round roast

3 green bell peppers, seeded and chopped

2 cups chopped onion

1 clove garlic, minced

½ cup brown sugar

3 tablespoons chili powder

2 teaspoons salt

1 teaspoon dry mustard

1 cup barbecue sauce

¼ cup apple cider vinegar

2 teaspoons Worcestershire sauce

10 to 12 sandwich buns, for serving

Combine all ingredients in a large Dutch oven or roasting pan. Cook, covered, in a 350°F oven for 2 to 3 hours, or until beef is tender and shreds easily with a fork. (I put mine in the oven, but the beef can also be cooked in a crock pot on high heat for 3 to 4 hours.) Serve on sandwich buns.

IN FIELD AND STREAM

*H*unting for mushrooms is always a fun thing for me. I love to eat mushrooms that have been rolled in flour and fried in butter or cooked on the grill. Mushrooms are a delicacy and aren't around for very long, so you need to look for them at the right time. The warm spring rains are great for bringing out wild mushrooms. Some years the conditions for mushroom hunting are better than others.

When I was a child, my dad would take me along to hunt mushrooms. He would show me which ones were okay to eat and which ones were poisonous. A good thunderstorm in warming spring weather was ideal for a mushroom hunt. Dad taught me that the flat mushrooms that grow around trees are poisonous. The ones we mostly hunt for are spikes and yellow sponges that grow around stumps. Morels are a tasty mushroom and are more easily found here in Michigan than where I grew up.

—Husband Joe

My husband Tim is a hunter. He hunts white deer. We enjoy the venison meat for jerky, summer sausage, ground meat, canned venison chunks, steaks, and snack sticks. Tim would like to try making bratwursts this year with a buck he recently harvested.

Our children enjoy taking turns going out and hunting with Tim. He built two deer blinds this summer to have a better place to sit when the children are along. This way the children can be free to move around a little more and he can still hunt effectively.

—Daughter Elizabeth

Here in Michigan, deer are plentiful, and lots of hunting occurs when the deer hunting season is open. Some in our family hunt with bow or gun or both. Lots of our freezers are filled with venison. Son-in-law Tim made a deer hunting shack higher up and built a ramp going up to it so our children who use mobility scooters can get up there to hunt as well. That was very thoughtful of him. We have made a lot of summer sausage and jerky from the harvested deer.

Joe and son Kevin went walleye fishing when we went to the Outer Banks one year with Joe's employer. Son Benjamin also loves going on fishing trips for walleye or salmon. Fishing is quite common around here with all the lakes we have close by. The most common fish we catch in our area are blue gills, bass, and perch. We often go on the boat or pontoon to fish. I am not into fishing, but I like going along to sit on the water and relax and sometimes read. Joe loves to take a portable grill along to have a small picnic on the pontoon.

—Lovina

SALMON PATTIES

Makes 4 to 6 servings

We frequently fix salmon on the grill. On the rare occasion that we have leftovers, this is a great way to use up leftover cooked salmon. Son Benjamin enjoys going salmon fishing with some of his friends and keeps us well supplied.

1 (15½-ounce) can salmon or 2 cups cooked salmon
1 cup crushed round buttery crackers
1 small onion, diced
¼ cup diced green bell pepper or celery
1 egg, beaten
1 teaspoon salt
½ teaspoon garlic salt
Pepper, as desired
All-purpose flour, for dipping

Combine all the ingredients except the flour, in a large bowl, mixing well. The salmon mixture should be slightly moist and should hold together when shaped into a ball. If not, add another egg. Form the mixture into 6 to 8 evenly sized patties, dip in flour, and fry in a medium-hot skillet lightly coated with oil until golden brown on each side.

BAKED FISH

Makes 4 servings

We love going fishing on the pontoon or boat during the warmer months. Often we will bring a small grill along and cook some sort of meat while fishing—right on the pontoon. Bass and bluegill are what we catch most. If you don't have access to walleye, any mild whitefish can work, such as cod, tilapia, or halibut.

6 to 8 tablespoons butter, melted

1 tablespoon lemon juice

Salt and pepper, as desired

4 (⅓-pound) fillets walleyed pike (about 1⅓ pounds total)

⅓ cup sliced fresh white button or cremini mushrooms

2 tablespoons chopped onion

Preheat the oven to 350°F.

Combine melted butter, lemon juice, and salt and pepper in a shallow baking dish. Dip fish in butter mixture so both sides are coated, then place filets in a shallow baking pan. Place mushrooms and onions over the top of the fish, then spoon remaining butter mixture over fish. Bake for 15 to 20 minutes; fish will flake easily when it is cooked through.

BAKED VENISON AND BEEF BURGERS

Makes 4 to 6 servings

We usually grill or fry our burgers, but baking is another reliable way to prepare them. The ground beef mixed in with the venison makes for some juicy burgers. If you don't have venison, you can double the amount of beef listed here. We also like to add in some shredded Colby or Colby Jack cheese with the burger mixture before baking for all-in-one cheeseburgers.

¾ cup rolled oats

¾ cup milk

¼ cup chopped onion

1 egg, beaten

½ to 1 teaspoon seasoned salt (use the smaller amount if you prefer your burgers less salty)

1 pound ground venison

1 pound ground beef

⅓ cup ketchup

1 tablespoon brown sugar

1 tablespoon Worcestershire sauce

1 tablespoon prepared yellow mustard

Hamburger buns, for serving

Toppings such as lettuce leaves, pickles, sliced onions, and sliced tomatoes, for serving

Combine oats, milk, onion, egg, and seasoned salt in a large bowl. Add the venison (if using) and beef and mix together. Shape the mixture into 6 evenly sized patties. Place the patties in a greased 13 x 9-inch baking pan with a little space between each patty. Mix ketchup, brown sugar, Worcestershire sauce, and mustard. Spoon over patties. Bake, uncovered, at 350°F for 22 to 26 minutes, or until juice runs clear. Serve on toasted hamburger buns and with burger toppings as desired.

VENISON OR BEEF JERKY

Jerky made from venison or beef is a favorite snack around here. During hunting season, our dehydrator is put to good use regularly making jerky.

2 pounds venison or beef bottom roast, brisket, or flank steak
¼ cup soy sauce
1 tablespoon Worcestershire sauce
1½ tablespoons liquid smoke
1 teaspoon salt
¼ teaspoon garlic powder
¼ teaspoon onion powder

Cut meat into strips 1 inch wide by ¼ to ⅜ inch thick. Remove all fat.

Mix together the remaining ingredients in a large glass dish with a lid. Place meat in marinade and cover tightly. Refrigerate 10 to 12 hours, stirring every 3 to 4 hours. Pat meat dry on paper towels; discard paper towels. Dehydrate strips on a rack in the oven with the oven set at the lowest temperature for 4 to 6 hours, until meat is firm. (Place a sheet pan under the rack to catch drips.) Or use a food dehydrator, putting the marinated meat in trays. After 12 hours, rotate trays. Continue until meat is fully dried. The jerky keeps well when frozen; simply thaw before eating.

Savoring
a Moment
COOKIES, BARS, AND OTHER TREATS

SUGAR COOKIES

Makes 7 dozen cookies

Son-in-law Ervin shared his mom's sugar cookie recipe with me. Sugar cookies are often passed around during church with crackers and pretzels for the little children to nibble on. These can be sprinkled with colored sugar before baking or frosted after. We often add chocolate chips to the dough before baking.

3 cups granulated sugar

2 cups shortening

5 eggs, beaten

1⅓ cups milk

1 tablespoon vanilla extract

8½ cups all-purpose flour

4 heaping teaspoons baking powder

1 teaspoon baking soda

1 teaspoon cream of tartar

1 teaspoon salt

Preheat the oven to 400°F. Mix together the ingredients in the order given. (If you prefer a softer cookie, first cream together the sugar, shortening, and eggs until light and fluffy. Whisk together the dry ingredients and then add to the creamed sugar mixture.)

Drop the dough by tablespoonfuls onto a greased baking sheet. Bake at 400°F for 8 to 10 minutes, or until the edges are browned. Using a spatula, remove the cookies one by one from the baking sheet and place on a wire rack to cool completely.

FROSTED RHUBARB COOKIES

Makes 4 dozen cookies

Even if you don't care for the taste of rhubarb, I think you might still love this cookie. The cream cheese frosting finishes it off with a delicious flavor.

1 cup (2 sticks) butter or shortening
1½ cups firmly packed light brown sugar
2 large eggs, beaten
3 cups all-purpose flour
1 teaspoon baking soda
½ teaspoon salt
1½ cups diced fresh rhubarb

Frosting
3 ounces cream cheese, softened
1 tablespoon butter, softened
1 tablespoon vanilla extract
1½ cups powdered sugar

Preheat the oven to 350°F.

In a medium mixing bowl, cream together the butter and brown sugar until smooth. Add the eggs one at a time, stirring until well combined. In another large bowl, sift together the flour, baking soda, and salt. Add the flour mixture to the batter, and beat until smooth. Fold in rhubarb until the ingredients are evenly combined.

Drop the batter by tablespoons onto an ungreased baking sheet. Bake cookies until lightly browned, 12 to 13 minutes. Using a spatula, remove the cookies one by one from the baking sheet and place on a wire rack to cool completely before frosting.

Make the frosting: In a small bowl, beat together the cream cheese, butter, and vanilla until smooth. Gradually add the powdered sugar until the frosting reaches the consistency that you prefer. Frost the cookies.

MONSTER COOKIES

Makes 3 dozen cookies

Monster cookies are one of our family's favorite cookies. Add the smaller amount of oats for a softer cookie; for a firmer and crispier cookie, use the larger amount.

3 eggs
1¼ cups firmly packed light brown sugar
1 cup granulated sugar
1 (12-ounce) jar creamy peanut butter
½ cup (1 stick) butter, softened
½ teaspoon vanilla extract
½ teaspoon salt
½ cup mini candy-coated chocolate pieces
½ cup chocolate chips
2 teaspoons baking soda
3½ to 4 cups quick-cooking oats (not instant)

Preheat the oven to 350°F. Line baking sheets with parchment paper or non-stick baking mats. In a very large bowl, combine the eggs and both sugars. Mix well. Add peanut butter, butter, vanilla, and salt; mix well. Stir in the candy-coated chocolate pieces, chocolate chips, baking soda, and oats. Drop the batter by tablespoonfuls 2 inches apart onto the prepared baking sheet.

Bake for 8 to 10 minutes. Do not overbake. Let cookies stand on the baking tray for about 3 minutes before transferring them to a wire rack to cool.

LUNCHROOM BROWNIES

Makes 1 dozen large brownies

These are a favorite in our house and don't last long when everyone comes home. We usually don't frost our brownies, but I've included a frosting recipe in case you prefer them that way. They're delicious served warm with ice cream or milk.

1 cup (2 sticks) butter
½ cup cocoa powder
2 cups all-purpose flour
2 cups granulated sugar
4 eggs, beaten
4 teaspoons vanilla extract
1 cup chopped walnuts (optional)

Frosting (optional)
¼ cup (½ stick) butter, softened
¼ cup whole milk
¼ cup cocoa powder
3 cups powdered sugar
Dash salt

In a large bowl, mix together brownie ingredients in the order listed. Pour the batter into a greased 13 x 9-inch baking pan, and bake at 350°F for 20 to 25 minutes, checking for doneness at 20 minutes. Brownies are done when the edges have pulled away from the sides of the pan and a toothpick inserted in the center comes out clean. Cool the brownies completely before frosting.

Make frosting: In a medium bowl, mix together ingredients in the order listed. Use additional milk to thin the frosting to your preferred consistency. Frost the cooled brownies in the pan.

CHOCOLATE PEANUT BUTTER BARS

Makes 12 to 16 bars

The combination of chocolate and peanut butter makes this bar extra tasty. It's great for a snack or dessert and perfect to pack in lunches.

2 cups quick-cooking oats
1¾ cups firmly packed brown sugar
1½ cups all-purpose flour
1 teaspoon baking powder
½ teaspoon baking soda
1 cup (2 sticks) butter
½ cup chopped peanuts
1 large egg, beaten
1 (14-ounce) can sweetened condensed milk
½ cup creamy peanut butter
1 cup (6 ounces) semisweet chocolate chips

Preheat the oven to 350°F. Combine oats, brown sugar, flour, baking powder, and baking soda in a large bowl. Cut in butter with a pastry blender or two knives until the mixture resembles fine crumbs. Stir in chopped peanuts.

Reserve 1½ cups of the crumb mixture. Stir egg into remaining crumb mixture. Press crust mixture onto the bottom of a 13 x 9-inch baking pan. Bake for 15 minutes.

Stir together sweetened condensed milk and peanut butter in a small bowl until well combined. Pour evenly over partially baked crust.

Stir together reserved crumb mixture and chocolate chips. Sprinkle evenly over the peanut butter layer. Bake for an additional 15 minutes until golden brown. Cool in the pan before cutting into bars.

TOFFEE NUT BARS

Makes 2 dozen bars

This is a delicious bar to take to a coffee break, or just to have on hand for a treat.

Crust
½ cup (1 stick) butter, softened
½ cup packed brown sugar
1 cup all-purpose flour

Topping
2 large eggs
1 cup packed brown sugar
1 teaspoon vanilla extract
2 tablespoons all-purpose flour
1 teaspoon baking powder
½ teaspoon salt
1 cup unsweetened shredded coconut
¾ cup slivered almonds

Preheat the oven to 350°F.

Make the crust: In a small bowl, stir together the butter, brown sugar, and flour until the ingredients are evenly mixed. Press and flatten by hand into the bottom of an ungreased 13 x 9-inch baking pan. Bake for 10 to 12 minutes, checking for firmness at 10 minutes.

Make the topping: While the crust is baking, beat the eggs in a large bowl and then stir in the brown sugar, vanilla, flour, baking powder, salt, coconut, and almonds. When the crust is firm after baking for 10 to 12 minutes, remove the pan from the oven and spread the topping evenly over the crust. Be careful not to tear the crust. Return pan to the oven and continue baking until the topping is golden brown, 23 to 25 minutes. Watch carefully, as the top will easily burn. Cut into bars while still warm.

Store the cooled bars in a sealed container or cake safe. These should stay fresh for 3 to 4 days.

FAVORITE FAMILY MOMENTS

Even as a mother of two children, I surprisingly sometimes find free time, but not for long. Free time occurs after I lay the children down for their naps. I like to try to get caught up with work around the house, or then I will read or write—mostly write. Sometimes I take a nap with the children to rest while I can.

When my husband, Dustin, gets home from work, he takes charge of the children and plays with them awhile too. I'd say I get more free time when I take the children to Mom's. It's not just me there; more people are available to help me with the kids.

My favorite time of the day is when Dustin and I gather both boys to sit down for a meal. Oldest son Denzel sits in a high step stool with a set where he can reach his own plate to eat. Denzel is starting to copy everything we do. When we bow our heads to pray before and after eating, he does it too. Every time we cough or sneeze, we can hear him mimicking us. We sit younger son Byron in a baby seat on top of the table, and Denzel likes it when he can get Byron to giggle in response to what he does. My favorite time of the day is when we are all together as a family.

I want my children to grow up and remember living in a home filled with the love of family where they also learned about God's great love—just like how Dustin and I were raised.

—Daughter Loretta

One year for my birthday and Christmas gift, my husband Joe and our children presented me with a nice oak rolltop desk made by a man in our community. I have it in my living room, and hardly a day goes by that I don't sit at that desk writing. Perhaps I am paying bills, writing to a friend, signing a card, or writing my weekly newspaper column. I love this desk. It was a wonderful, thoughtful, and useful gift that will last a lifetime. I will always treasure it. Then maybe some day in future years, it can be passed down to another family member, making more memories.

—Lovina

RHUBARB DREAM BARS

Makes 20 bars

This bar recipe tastes similar to rhubarb custard pie. We have plenty of rhubarb in our garden during the spring and early summer months, so we make these more often then.

Crust
2 cups all-purpose flour
¾ cup powdered sugar
1 cup (2 sticks) butter, softened

Filling
4 eggs, beaten
2 cups granulated sugar
¼ cup all-purpose flour
½ teaspoon salt
2 cups chopped rhubarb (½-inch pieces)

Prepare the crust: Mix together crust ingredients and press into a 13 x 9-inch baking pan. Preheat the oven to 350°F.

Prepare the filling: In a large bowl, whisk together eggs and granulated sugar. Stir in flour and salt. Fold in rhubarb and combine well, then pour filling over crust in pan. Bake at 350°F for 45 to 60 minutes, or until set. The bars should be firm and not move when you shake the pan slightly.

PUMPKIN PIE SQUARES

Makes 16 squares

We make these pumpkin pie squares in the fall when the pumpkins are in season. Like pumpkin pie, they taste best served with a dollop of whipped cream.

Crust
½ cup butter, softened
½ cup brown sugar
1 cup all-purpose flour
½ cup rolled oats

Crumb topping
½ cup brown sugar
2 tablespoons butter, softened

Filling
2 eggs
¾ cup granulated sugar
½ cup all-purpose flour
1 (15-ounce) can pumpkin puree
1½ cups whole milk
½ teaspoon salt
1 teaspoon ground cinnamon
½ teaspoon ground ginger (optional)
¼ teaspoon ground nutmeg (optional)

Make crust: Preheat the oven to 350°F. Mix together butter and brown sugar, then mix in flour and oats to make an oatmeal crumble crust. Press crust in a 13 x 9-inch baking dish. Bake at 350°F for 15 minutes. (Remove the pan from the oven but don't turn off the oven.)

Make filling and crumb topping: While the crust is baking, prepare the filling ingredients: In a large bowl, beat the eggs and mix in the granulated sugar and flour. Whisk in pumpkin and milk. Mix in salt and cinnamon, and ginger and nutmeg, if using. In a small bowl, mix together the brown sugar and the butter. When the crust is finished baking, pour the filling over the hot crust. Sprinkle the crumb topping over the filling.

Return the pan to the oven and bake for an additional 20 minutes until set. Let cool before cutting into squares. If desired, serve with a spoonful of whipped topping on each piece.

FROSTY STRAWBERRY SQUARES

Makes 10 to 12 squares

These make a great snack on a hot summer day since it's served cold. The bars need to stay frozen, and should only be brought out of the freezer right before serving. It may take longer to whip pasteurized egg whites, but adding a little lemon juice or cream of tartar shortly into the whipping process will help the whites take shape.

4 tablespoons pasteurized liquid egg white (equivalent to 2 egg whites)
1 cup granulated sugar
¼ teaspoon cream of tartar, or ½ teaspoon lemon juice (optional)
2 cups fresh strawberries, hulled and crushed
1 cup whipping cream

In a large bowl, combine the egg whites and sugar. Whip for 1 minute. When the mixture starts to become foamy, add the cream of tartar or lemon juice, if using. Continue whipping for 10 minutes or longer, until the mixture has doubled or tripled in size. (Pasteurized egg whites take longer to whip up.) Gently stir the crushed strawberries into the egg mixture.

In a separate bowl, beat the whipping cream until stiff peaks form. Carefully fold the whipped cream into the strawberry mixture until well blended. Pour into an ungreased 13 x 9-inch rectangular cake pan. Freeze until firm, at least 6 hours. Cut into squares and serve.

LEMON SQUARES

Makes 16 squares

This is a refreshing bar on a hot summer day. If you like the tart flavor of lemon, these will quickly become a favorite.

Crust
1¼ cups powdered sugar
½ cup all-purpose flour
Pinch salt
½ cup (1 stick) plus 1 tablespoon
    butter

Filling
2 large eggs, slightly beaten
¼ cup fresh lemon juice
1 cup granulated sugar
½ teaspoon baking powder

Glaze
¾ cup powdered sugar, sifted
2 tablespoons fresh lemon juice
1 tablespoon butter, melted

Preheat the oven to 350°F. Line an 8 x 8-inch cake pan with parchment paper. Make sure an inch of paper overlaps the edges so that the bars can be lifted out when they are done.

Make the crust: In a large bowl, combine the powdered sugar, flour, salt, and butter together until dry, coarse crumbs form. Press firmly into an even layer in the prepared pan. Bake for 15 minutes. Let cool for a few minutes before adding the filling. (You may want to keep the oven on for the next step.)

Make the filling: Whisk together the eggs, lemon juice, granulated sugar, and baking powder in a bowl until the sugar has completely dissolved. Pour over the crust. Bake at 350°F until the filling is nearly set but jiggles a little, 25 to 30 minutes. Let cool completely.

Make the glaze: In a small bowl, mix the powdered sugar, lemon juice, and butter until evenly blended. Pour over the cooled filling. Let cool to room temperature. Lift from the pan and cut into bars.

    Store the bars in a sealed container or cake safe. These should stay fresh for 3 to 4 days.

BIG APPLE FRITTERS

Makes 4 servings

This is an easy recipe to make when you have apples on hand. When we go to the local orchard to pick grapes for grape juice, we usually purchase several bushels of apples. We store them on our back porch to keep them cool.

2 cups all-purpose flour

2 tablespoons granulated sugar

2 teaspoons baking powder

½ teaspoon salt

1 cup milk

1 large egg

1 teaspoon vanilla extract

2 medium apples, peeled and diced

Vegetable oil, for frying

Powdered sugar, for dusting

In a large bowl, whisk together the flour, sugar, baking powder, and salt. In a separate bowl, whisk together the milk, egg, and vanilla extract. Add the egg mixture to the flour mixture and mix until combined. Gently fold the diced apples into the batter.

Heat about 2 inches of vegetable oil in a large saucepan or Dutch oven over medium-high heat until a deep-fry thermometer reads 375°F. Line a plate with a paper towel.

Drop spoonfuls of the fritter batter into the hot oil, being careful not to overcrowd the pan. Cook the fritter for 2 to 3 minutes, or until golden brown. Using a slotted spoon, transfer the fritters to a paper towel–lined plate to drain.

Dust the fritters with powdered sugar while still warm. Enjoy!

DOUGHNUTS

Makes about 3 dozen doughnuts

Doughnuts are something we like to make fresh on butchering day mornings. They are wonderful served with coffee or milk. To prepare the scalded milk, heat the milk to just below boiling, then cool to room temperature.

½ cup scalded milk

½ cup granulated sugar

2 teaspoons salt

2 cups lukewarm water

2 packages (1¼-ounces each) yeast

2 eggs, beaten

½ cup shortening or butter, melted

7½ to 8 cups all-purpose flour

Vegetable oil, for frying

White vinegar

Granulated sugar (optional)

Glaze (optional)

2 cups powdered sugar

¼ cup boiling water

Mix together scalded milk, sugar, and salt in a large bowl. Dissolve the yeast in 2 cups lukewarm water, then add to the milk mixture. Add the beaten eggs and melted shortening. Last, mix in 7 cups of the flour and only add the rest if needed. Do not mix in too much flour—the dough should be as soft as possible, almost too sticky to handle.

Let the dough rise for half an hour. Punch it down, then let it rise for another half hour. Roll out the dough about ½ inch thick, cut out doughnuts, and shape into circles with a hole in the center. Let rise for 15 to 20 minutes until ready to fry.

Pour oil into a heavy saucepan to a depth of ½ to ¾ inch and heat over medium-high heat until a deep-fry thermometer reads 365°F. To keep the grease from soaking into the fried doughnuts, add several tablespoons of vinegar to the oil before frying. Fry doughnuts until golden brown on each side, turning once with a long tongs or fork. Remove the doughnuts from oil with a slotted spoon. Roll hot doughnuts in sugar, or dip in glaze prepared by mixing together powdered sugar and boiling water.

Celebrating
Something Sweet
CAKES, PIES, AND OTHER DESSERTS

CINNAMON ROLL COFFEE CAKE

Makes 12 servings

If you like cinnamon rolls, then you will love this cake! It's fairly easy to make, and is a great item to serve at a family dinner, coffee break, or other event.

Cake
½ cup (1 stick) butter, melted
1½ cups milk
2 eggs, beaten
3 cups all-purpose flour
1 cup granulated sugar
4 teaspoons baking powder
¼ teaspoon salt
2 teaspoons vanilla extract

Topping
1 cup (2 sticks) butter, melted
1 cup brown sugar
2 tablespoons all-purpose flour
1 tablespoon cinnamon

Glaze
2 cups powdered sugar
5 tablespoons milk
1 teaspoon vanilla extract

Preheat the oven to 350°F.

Prepare cake: In a large bowl, mix together all the cake ingredients until well combined. Pour into a greased 13 x 9-inch baking pan.

Prepare topping: Whisk together all the topping ingredients in a small bowl until well combined. Spread topping evenly over the batter in the pan and swirl with a knife. Bake at 350°F for 30 to 35 minutes, or until a toothpick inserted in the center comes out clean.

Prepare glaze: While the cake bakes, mix together all the glaze ingredients in a small bowl until it's the consistency of maple syrup. Drizzle the glaze over the cake while it is still warm, and it will set into a harder glaze. Serve slices of the cake warm or at room temperature.

FRESH APPLE CAKE

Makes 12 to 16 servings

We eat a lot of apples with popcorn and a glass of fresh cider during the fall. This is a favorite snack on a chilly night or Sunday afternoon.

3 cups all-purpose flour

1 teaspoon baking soda

1 teaspoon salt

2 teaspoons ground cinnamon

1 teaspoon ground cloves

1 teaspoon ground nutmeg

2 cups granulated sugar

1½ cups vegetable oil

3 eggs

1 teaspoon vanilla extract

3 cups peeled and chopped apples

1 cup pecan pieces

Topping

⅓ cup brown sugar

1 teaspoon ground cinnamon

Preheat the oven to 350°F.

Whisk together flour, baking soda, salt, and spices. Set aside. In a large bowl, combine granulated sugar, oil, eggs, and vanilla. Beat well. Add flour mixture to oil mixture in three portions along with half of the chopped apples, beating at medium speed. Fold in by hand the rest of the apples and the pecans. Pour batter into a greased and floured tube pan.

Make topping: Mix together the brown sugar and cinnamon in a small bowl. Sprinkle the topping over the batter. Bake at 350°F for 60 minutes, or until a toothpick inserted in the center comes out clean. Let cool completely before removing from the pan.

PUMPKIN ROLL

Makes 12 to 16 servings

We always serve pumpkin rolls as one of the desserts for our Thanksgiving dinner.

Cake

3 eggs, beaten

⅔ cup pumpkin puree

1 cup granulated sugar

¾ cup all-purpose flour

1 teaspoon baking soda

2 teaspoons ground cinnamon

1 teaspoon ground ginger

½ teaspoon ground nutmeg

½ teaspoon salt

Filling

1 cup powdered sugar

1 tablespoon butter, softened

1 (8-ounce) package cream cheese, softened to room temperature

1 teaspoon vanilla extract

Preheat the oven to 350°F. Combine the eggs, pumpkin, and granulated sugar in a large bowl, then add the flour, baking soda, spices, and salt, and blend together well. Pour the batter into a 15 x 10 x 1-inch greased baking sheet. Bake at 350°F for 15 minutes.

Sprinkle a clean kitchen towel with powdered sugar. When the pumpkin cake comes out of the oven, invert it onto the towel. Starting from the shorter side and keeping the kitchen towel tucked inside, roll up the cake like a jelly roll; let cool. (The towel helps the cake keep its shape without cracking; it will be removed after the cake has cooled and before you add the filling.)

Make the filling: Mix filling ingredients together in a medium bowl until smooth. Unroll cooled cake, remove towel, then spread the filling evenly over the cake. Working quickly, roll up the cake again without the towel and refrigerate until serving.

PUMPKIN WHOOPIE PIES

Makes 3 dozen sandwich pies

My husband Joe loves these whoopie pies with coffee in the morning before work or packed in his lunch. Sometimes I add a half cup of ground black walnuts to the batter, which gives these cookies added special flavor.

Cookies

2 cups packed brown sugar

1 cup vegetable oil

1½ cups cooked, mashed pumpkin
(can also use canned pumpkin
puree)

2 eggs

3 cups all-purpose flour

1 teaspoon salt

1 teaspoon baking powder

1 teaspoon baking soda

1 teaspoon vanilla extract

1½ tablespoons ground cinnamon

½ tablespoon ground ginger

½ tablespoon ground cloves

Filling

½ cup milk

1 (8-ounce) package cream cheese,
softened

3 to 4 cups powdered sugar

2 teaspoons vanilla extract

Preheat the oven to 350°F.

Cream together brown sugar and oil in a large bowl. Add pumpkin and eggs and mix together. Add flour, salt, baking powder, baking soda, vanilla, and spices. Mix well.

Drop by heaping teaspoonfuls onto a greased baking sheet. Bake at 350°F for 10 to 12 minutes. Cool cookies completely before adding filling.

Make filling: Mix together filling ingredients until smooth and spreadable. Spread a dollop of filling between two cookies, repeating with remaining filling and cookies. Any leftover filling can be stored, covered, in the refrigerator for several days.

RHUBARB SHORTCAKE

Makes 6 to 8 servings

My mother made this quite often when rhubarb was in season. I don't make this as much as she did, but it is still a delicious treat. My mother served it warm with cold milk poured over it.

4 cups all-purpose flour
1 teaspoon baking soda
2 teaspoons baking powder
Pinch salt
3 cups milk mixed with 1 tablespoon apple cider vinegar (let stand 5 minutes)
2 cups chopped rhubarb
1 cup granulated sugar

Preheat the oven to 350°F.

In a large bowl, combine the flour, baking soda, baking powder, and salt. Then gradually add the milk mixture until a really soft dough forms. Spread a layer of this dough in a greased 13 x 9-inch cake pan, and then add the rhubarb in a thick layer. Sprinkle the sugar evenly over the rhubarb. Spread the rest of the dough on top of the rhubarb and bake the cake until the rhubarb is tender, about 45 minutes.

SPICE CAKE

Makes 12 to 16 servings

You can use your favorite icing to frost this cake or just serve it plain. Our family prefers cream cheese frosting, as it goes well with the warming flavor of this spice cake. Check out Decorator's Cream Cheese Frosting (p. 111) for an option.

2 cups packed brown sugar

½ cup (1 stick) butter

2 eggs

2½ cups sifted all-purpose flour

1½ teaspoons baking powder

1 teaspoon baking soda

1 teaspoon ground cinnamon

1 teaspoon ground nutmeg

1 cup milk mixed with 1 teaspoon apple cider vinegar (let stand 5 minutes)

1 teaspoon vanilla extract

Preheat the oven to 350°F.

In a large bowl, cream together sugar and butter until fluffy. Add eggs and beat until the mixture is lighter. In a medium bowl, sift together the flour, baking powder, baking soda, cinnamon, and nutmeg. Alternate adding the flour mixture and the milk mixture to the egg mixture, beating well after each addition. Mix in the vanilla. Pour batter into two greased 8-inch layer pans or a greased 13 x 9-inch cake pan. Bake at 350°F for 35 to 40 minutes. If opting to frost the cake, wait to do so until it has cooled completely.

CHOCOLATE ZUCCHINI CAKE

Makes 12 to 16 servings

This cake is often on our family's menu during zucchini harvest time. It's a scrumptious way to use up surplus zucchini! The chocolate and zucchini go well together.

½ cup (1 stick) butter

½ cup vegetable oil

1¾ cups granulated sugar

2 eggs

½ cup milk mixed with ½ teaspoon apple cider vinegar (let stand 5 minutes)

1 tablespoon vanilla extract

2½ cups all-purpose flour

4 tablespoons cocoa powder

½ teaspoon baking powder

½ teaspoon baking soda

½ teaspoon salt

½ teaspoon ground cinnamon

½ teaspoon ground cloves

2 cups shredded zucchini

¼ cup chocolate chips

Preheat the oven to 350°F.

Cream together butter, oil, and sugar in a large bowl. Add eggs and milk mixture and beat well. Stir in the remaining ingredients except chocolate chips. Pour batter into a greased and floured Bundt or tube cake pan. Sprinkle chocolate chips on top. Bake at 350°F for 40 to 45 minutes.

CHOCOLATE SHEET CAKE

Makes 24 servings

This cake works well to take along for a lot of occasions, including a potluck or family reunion. You can also decorate it as a birthday cake. The grandchildren like it even better when we add sprinkles.

Cake

2 cups all-purpose flour

2 cups granulated sugar

¼ teaspoon salt

1 cup (2 sticks) butter

4 heaping tablespoons cocoa powder

1 cup boiling water

½ cup buttermilk

2 eggs, beaten

1 teaspoon baking soda

2 teaspoons vanilla extract

Frosting

¾ cup (1½ sticks) butter

4 heaping tablespoons cocoa powder

6 tablespoons milk

2 teaspoons vanilla extract

3 cups powdered sugar

Make the cake: Preheat the oven to 350°F. In a mixing bowl, combine flour, granulated sugar, and salt. Melt the butter in a saucepan, then add cocoa powder and mix together. Keeping the pan over medium heat, stir in boiling water, and allow the mixture to boil for 30 seconds. Remove from heat and pour the cocoa mixture over the flour mixture, stirring lightly to cool.

In a small bowl, whisk together the buttermilk, eggs, baking soda, and vanilla. Stir the buttermilk mixture into the chocolate mixture. Pour batter into a greased 17 x 12-inch half sheet pan and bake at 350°F for 20 minutes.

Make the frosting: While the cake is baking, melt butter in a medium saucepan. Add cocoa powder to the pan, stir to combine, then turn off the heat. Add the milk, vanilla, and powdered sugar. Stir together well until smooth, then pour over the warm cake in the pan. Top with sprinkles if desired.

CHOCOLATE ANGEL FOOD CAKE

Makes 12 to 16 servings

I prefer angel food cake to regular cake. Angel food cake is served at Amish weddings quite often. When I make homemade noodles, I only need the yolks. I use up the egg whites to make angel food cake.

¾ **cup cake flour**
¼ **cup cocoa powder**
¼ **teaspoon salt**
1 **teaspoon cream of tartar**
2 **cups egg whites (14 to 16 egg whites)**
1 **teaspoon vanilla extract**
1½ **cups granulated sugar**

Preheat the oven to 350°F.

Sift together flour, cocoa powder, and salt in a small bowl. In a large mixing bowl, blend the cream of tartar into the egg whites and beat them until they form soft peaks. Gently fold in the vanilla, then fold in the sugar a tablespoon at a time. Gradually fold the flour mixture into the whipped egg whites. Pour into an ungreased tube pan and bake at 350°F for 40 to 45 minutes, or until the top springs back when pressed firmly. When the cake is finished baking, invert on a wire rack to cool.

FRESH STRAWBERRY PIE

Makes 6 to 8 servings

Strawberry pie is often served at spring or early summer weddings when straw-berries are in season. This version uses one prebaked crust. My recipe for Pie Crust (p. 187) makes enough for three pie crusts. If you plan to make only one pie, the extra dough can be stored in the freezer.

When I was a young girl, a few of my sisters and I worked at a strawberry U-pick farm. There were rows and rows of strawberries that needed to be picked for the farmer to sell. We sorted the good, ripe berries from the ones with spots, also known as "seconds"; we could take those home. The seconds always supplied my mother with her strawberries for the season. We were paid per each bucket of good strawberries we picked. I was thrilled because it was my first paid job.

½ **cup granulated sugar**
3 tablespoons cornstarch
2 tablespoons light corn syrup
1 cup water
3 tablespoons strawberry-flavored gelatin
Red food color (optional)
6 cups fresh strawberries, hulled and sliced
1 (9-inch) baked pie crust, cooled or at room temperature

Make the filling: Combine the sugar, cornstarch, corn syrup, and water in a large saucepan and bring mixture to a boil. Boil, stirring constantly, until thickened, about 5 minutes.

Remove from heat. Stir in the gelatin and a few drops of red food color, if desired. Let cool until lukewarm. Add the strawberries, stir to coat the berries, and then pour into the baked crust. Refrigerate pie for 2 hours before serving. Serve with whipped cream, if desired.

STRAWBERRY RHUBARB PIE

Makes 6 to 8 servings

This lovely pie is pictured on the cover of this cookbook. Rhubarb and straw-berries make a great flavor combination and a delicious dessert. You will need enough pie pastry to make a crust and lattice top for a 9-inch pie. See my recipe for Pie Crust (p. 187), which yields three pie pastries. The extra dough can be frozen or used for a separate single-crust pie.

I use a lattice pie top cutter, but you can also weave a lattice top from strips of pie pastry. First, roll out pastry into a 10-inch circle. Cut the dough into even strips, ½ to ¾ inch wide, using a knife or pastry wheel. You should have about a dozen strips.

When you are ready to top your pie, lay half of the strips in parallel rows over the filling, leaving about a ½ inch of space between each strip. Gently fold back every other strip. Weave in the cross strips: Place a long strip of dough perpen-dicular to the parallel strips. Unfold the folded strips over the perpendicular one. Then take the parallel strips that are underneath the perpendicular one and fold them back over it. Place a second perpendicular strip next to the first one, leav-ing some space between them, then unfold the folded strips over the second one. Continue this process until the weave is complete. Trim the edges flush with the dough in the bottom of the pan, then seal and crimp the edges.

Weaving a lattice top is not too difficult once you get the hang of it, but you can see why I use a lattice cutter!

3 eggs, beaten

1¼ cups granulated sugar

¼ cup all-purpose flour

¼ teaspoon salt

½ teaspoon ground nutmeg

2½ cups chopped rhubarb (1-inch pieces)

1½ cups hulled and sliced fresh strawberries

2 (9-inch) pie pastries (one for the crust and one for the lattice top)

1 tablespoon butter, cut into small pieces

Combine eggs, sugar, flour, salt, and nutmeg in a bowl; mix well. In a separate bowl, combine rhubarb and strawberries. On a lightly floured surface, roll out one of the pie pastries large enough to line a 9-inch pie plate. Line the plate with the pastry and let the edges hang over the side; fill with fruit mixture.

Pour egg mixture over fruit mixture. Dot the pie filling with butter. Roll out the other pie pastry and cut into a lattice shape or cut into strips to weave a lattice top (see note). Top pie with lattice pastry, trimming the edges as needed. Seal the bottom crust and lattice together by crimping the edges high.

Bake at 400°F for about 40 minutes, or until crust is browned and the filling is bubbling.

GREEN GRAPE PIE

Makes 6 to 8 servings

This unique pie may not be as popular as other pies on my family's table, but I like to rotate pies for a change of taste. You will need one pie pastry for a 9-inch pie. My recipe for Pie Crust (p. 187) will make enough for three pie pastries; you can freeze the extra dough for several months.

1 quart seedless green grapes

½ cup granulated sugar

¼ teaspoon salt

⅛ teaspoon nutmeg

½ teaspoon grated lemon rind or juice

1 teaspoon grated orange rind, or 2 tablespoons orange juice concentrate

1 (9-inch) pie pastry

1 tablespoon butter, cut into small pieces

Preheat the oven to 425°F.

Cut half of the grapes in two, leaving the rest whole. Mix all the ingredients together in a large bowl and let stand for 15 to 20 minutes. Meanwhile, roll out the pie pastry on a lightly floured surface and line a 9-inch pie plate. Crimp the edges of the pie crust.

Fill the pie pastry with the fruit mixture. Dot with butter and bake at 425°F for 40 to 45 minutes, or until crust is browned and the filling is bubbling.

PIE CRUST

Makes 3 (9-inch) pie pastries

This go-to pastry crust recipe works well for making prebaked and baked crusts. Unused dough can be stored in disks in the freezer.

3 cups all-purpose flour
1 teaspoon salt
1 cup lard or shortening
1 egg
⅓ cup cold water
1 tablespoon apple cider vinegar

Combine flour and salt in a large bowl. Add lard or shortening and mix it into the flour with a fork or your fingers until the mixture resembles coarse crumbs. Add the egg, water, and vinegar, and stir with a fork until the mixture comes together.

Divide the dough into three equal parts and form each part into a ball. To use part of the recipe now, form one ball into a disk and roll it onto a floured surface to ⅛ inch thickness. Fit the dough into a 9-inch pie pan and trim the edges. For a prebaked crust, bake at 450°F for 10 to 12 minutes, or until lightly browned.

If not using the other two crusts, form the remaining two balls into disks and place in resealable plastic bags. The dough can be frozen up to 3 months. Thaw at least 12 hours in the refrigerator before baking.

APPLE DUMPLINGS

Makes 7 servings

When I was a young girl, my mother often made these for supper. She would serve them warm, and we would pour cold milk over the dumplings before eating. We never had a refrigerator or freezer at home, so we used a cooler with an ice block to keep food cold in the warm months. In the winter we would just set the food on a table in the enclosed but unheated back porch/entryway.

Any cooking apple works well for this recipe. We love to use McIntosh, Golden Delicious, Red Delicious, or Gala apples.

2 cups all-purpose flour
¾ cup shortening
1 teaspoon salt
2 teaspoons baking powder
½ cup milk
¼ cup (½ stick) butter
½ cup brown sugar
½ teaspoon ground cinnamon
¼ teaspoon ground nutmeg
7 medium apples, peeled, halved, and cored
Additional brown sugar and ground cinnamon, for sprinkling

Preheat the oven to 375°F. In a large bowl, mix together the flour, shortening, salt, baking powder, and milk as you would to make pie dough; set aside. In a small saucepan over medium heat, stir together ½ cup water, butter, brown sugar, cinnamon, and nutmeg. Heat just until the butter is melted.

Divide the dough into 14 even pieces and roll out into roughly formed squares large enough to wrap around an apple half. Wrap apple halves with dough. Gently press the dough together to seal. Put wrapped apple halves in an ungreased 13 x 9-inch baking pan seam side down. Pour the butter mixture over all the dumplings. Bake at 375°F until the pastry is brown, 25 to 30 minutes. Sprinkle with additional brown sugar and cinnamon to serve.

Welcoming Children

DISHES FOR YOUNG COOKS

YUMMY FILLED EGGS

Makes 2 dozen filled egg halves

When we have excess eggs, I like to turn them into these filled eggs. Older eggs peel more easily after boiling, so I prefer to use those. If you only have fresh eggs, here's a good way to boil them so they peel nicely: Place the eggs in a large saucepan, cover with water, and bring to a boil. Boil the eggs, uncovered, for two minutes. Then turn off the heat and let them sit, still covered, for eleven minutes. Drain the hot water and run cold water over the eggs.

1 dozen eggs
1 tablespoon salt
3 heaping tablespoons mayonnaise
2 teaspoons granulated sugar
2 dashes salt and pepper
2 teaspoons apple cider vinegar
2 dashes Worcestershire sauce
2 teaspoons prepared yellow mustard

Place the eggs in a large saucepan. Cover eggs with water and add 1 tablespoon salt. Bring pan to a boil and boil for 10 minutes. Drain the eggs and allow to cool to room temperature. Peel cooled eggs and cut in half lengthwise. Scoop out the yolks with a fork and mash them together in a mixing bowl. Add the remaining ingredients to the yolks, mixing thoroughly. Scoop a rounded tablespoon of filling into each egg half and enjoy.

DILL PICKLE PINWHEELS

Makes 12 servings

We often make this snack for a Christmas or Thanksgiving gathering. We usually have our main Thanksgiving meal around noon and Christmas brunch in the late morning. Then we have a variety of snacks later on instead of another full meal. This is a tasty and savory snack to counterbalance the many sweets served at special gatherings.

2 (8-ounce) packages cream cheese, softened
1 cup shredded cheese (Colby or any other semi-hard or hard cheese)
1 cup finely chopped dill pickles
1 cup chopped ham
1 (1-ounce) packet dry ranch seasoning
12 medium flour tortillas

In a large bowl, mix together cream cheese, shredded cheese, pickles, ham, and ranch seasoning until well combined. Spread a portion of the mixture onto a tortilla, leaving just a small border along the edge. Roll up the tortilla and cut into slices. Repeat with remaining filling and tortillas. You can also use the filling as a dip and serve it with crackers—another favorite variation in our house.

DEEP DISH TACO SQUARES

Makes 6 servings

I remember the first time I tasted these when I was a young girl. My sister-in-law Nancy had made them, and I loved them so much that I began making them quite often.

2 pounds ground beef

5 teaspoons taco seasoning (may measure out from two 1-ounce packets)

1 cup sour cream

⅔ cups whipped salad dressing

2½ cups shredded cheddar cheese

2 tablespoons onion, chopped

2 cups Quick Baking Mix (p. 55), made with butter

½ cup cold water

1 fresh tomato, cubed and seeded

½ cup chopped green bell pepper

Paprika, for sprinkling (optional)

In a large skillet, cook ground beef until brown. Drain the fat, then mix taco seasoning into the cooked ground beef. In a medium bowl, mix together sour cream, salad dressing, cheese, and onion. In a separate bowl, mix together the baking mix and water until a soft dough forms. Pat dough into a greased 13 x 9-inch baking pan, pressing the dough halfway up the sides. Layer beef, tomatoes, and bell peppers on the dough in the pan. Spoon sour cream mixture on top. Sprinkle with paprika, if desired. Bake at 375°F for 25 to 30 minutes.

PARTY MIX

Makes about 40 (½-cup) servings

We make this snack mix often around the holidays. You can add other ingredients of your choice or omit any components that don't suit your family's flavor preferences. We like to add roasted garlic rye chips.

4 cups wheat squares cereal

4 cups corn squares cereal

4 cups rice squares cereal

4 cups toasted oats cereal

4 cups pretzels (add more if desired)

3 cups peanuts or cashews (or a combination)

⅔ cup butter

1 teaspoon celery salt

2 tablespoons Worcestershire sauce

Mix together cereals, pretzels, and nuts in a large bowl. Melt butter in a small saucepan, then add celery salt and Worcestershire sauce, mixing well. Pour the butter sauce over dry ingredients and stir well to coat. Bake in two or three ungreased 13 x 9-inch baking pans at 250°F for 40 to 50 minutes, stirring every 10 minutes.

CARING AND COOKING FOR CHILDREN

I have always loved taking care of children ever since I was a little girl. I now do a lot of babysitting, which I enjoy immensely. I have often been the "maid" for my sisters after they have a baby. Attending to the housework on their behalf is fun, but I always want to take care of the baby too. Several times I've told the parents to go and rest while I stay up with the baby. Some babies are a little fussier than others, but I love them all the same.

The day before Ervin and my sister Susan's wedding, I had eight children over for the whole day—four boys and four girls. I gave all the boys a haircut and then bathed them. Then I bathed all the girls and washed their hair. Afterward we had supper.

Deciding on what meal to make has always been a struggle for me, and Mom was always the one who chose what to make for our family meals. But when I started working at a daycare, I had to come up with the meals myself. I would write down the meals we had on a whiteboard every day to keep track of what we ate. One little girl was allergic to peanut butter, so that was a specific ingredient I had to dodge. As time went on, I started to love planning meals.

Working at a daycare was fun and exhausting. I arrived early in the morning. Some of the children were already there, and others would still be arriving. We would have breakfast together, and then the children would play. Changing diapers remained a constant task as the morning went on. After lunch, I would change all of the children's diapers again. Then it would be nap time. It was so hard not to fall asleep with the kids; I had to keep busy doing something to stay awake. The workday would usually end around four or five in the evening. Children are so much fun, but it is also super tiring to care for twelve of them who are under seven years of age!

When my siblings and I all still lived at home, Saturdays were busy with everyone getting work done around the house. Every other Sunday was a church Sunday, and so on Saturday evenings, everyone would shower and wash their hair and prepare for the next day. We often made grilled cheese for supper because it was an easy meal to fix and allowed us to go to bed earlier the evening before church. I would write down everyone's grilled cheese order on a tablet. Some preferred Velveeta cheese; some preferred Colby. Some would want a hard-cooked egg in their grilled cheese, and some would want an egg over easy. It was so fun for me because I pretended I was working in a restaurant.

—Daughter Verena

DAUGHTER LOVINA'S GRIDDLE SANDWICH

Makes 1 sandwich

Daughter Lovina created this recipe after working at McDonald's. She had the job of making breakfast sandwiches there, which inspired her to cook something similar at home. Multiply the recipe as needed to make additional sandwiches.

2 pancakes (try Oatmeal Pancakes, p. 35; or pancakes made with Quick Baking Mix, p. 55)

1 cooked sausage patty, or 2 pieces fried bacon (or a combination of cooked breakfast meats)

1 fried egg, cooked well done

1 slice cheese of your choice

Pancake or maple syrup

Drizzle warm pancakes with syrup. Assemble a sandwich between the pancakes with sausage (or bacon), egg, and cheese. Serve with additional syrup, if desired.

DAUGHTER LOVINA'S BREAKFAST CRUNCH SANDWICH

Makes 1 serving

Daughter Lovina frequently makes this breakfast sandwich, which was inspired by the Crunchwrap from Taco Bell; everyone loves it when she makes these. We like to dip the sandwich in extra nacho cheese sauce. Multiply the recipe as needed to make additional servings.

2 to 3 tablespoons cheese sauce
1 large flour tortilla
1 hash brown patty, baked until crispy
1 sausage patty, fried
1 egg, scrambled
1 slice bacon, fried and cut in half
1 small flour tortilla

Spread a few tablespoons of cheese sauce in a circle over the middle of the large tortilla. Place the hash brown in the middle of the cheese sauce circle, then layer on the sausage, scrambled egg, and bacon pieces. Place the smaller tortilla over the top of the layers. Fold the large tortilla in toward the center and fold over the smaller tortilla so that all the filling layers are covered. Heat a small amount of oil in a medium-sized skillet. Place the sandwich in the skillet and brown the tortilla on both sides to make both tortillas brown and crispy.

COFFEE SOUP

Makes 4 to 6 servings

Coffee soup has been made in our family for many generations. We eat it most with ponhoss, also known as scrapple, after pork butchering day. Some of our children will drink coffee soup as a creamed coffee instead of adding toast or crackers.

2 cups brewed coffee

2 cups milk, or more as desired

½ cup granulated sugar, or more as desired

Toasted bread or saltine crackers, for serving

Combine all the ingredients in a saucepan and warm over medium heat until hot. Do not boil. Pour over toasted bread or saltine crackers.

FRUIT-FILLED OATMEAL SQUARES

Makes 2 dozen squares

This recipe works with a variety of flavors. You can choose your favorite pie filling instead of using the apple pie filling called for here. Some good alternatives include cherry or peach pie filling. My Homemade Fruit Pie Filling (p. 112) also works well here.

½ cup (1 stick) butter, softened

¼ cup all-purpose flour

1 cup packed brown sugar

1½ cups quick-cooking rolled oats

1 (21-ounce) can apple pie filling (or other fruit pie filling)

Preheat the oven to 350°F.

In a large bowl, combine the butter, flour, brown sugar, and oats until mixed evenly and the texture resembles coarse crumbs. Press two-thirds of the oat mixture into an ungreased 9 x 9-inch square baking pan. Pour the pie filling over the crust layer in the pan. Then sprinkle the remaining third of the oat mixture as crumbs on top. Bake until the oatmeal topping begins to turn golden brown, about 25 minutes. Cool completely and cut into squares.

Store the squares in a sealed container or cake safe. These should stay fresh for 3 to 4 days at room temperature.

NO-BAKE CHOCOLATE OATMEAL BARS

Makes 12 large or 24 small bars

These are simple to make when you need a quick, sweet snack. This was an easy recipe for my daughters to make on their own when they were younger because no baking is required.

1 cup (2 sticks) butter
½ cup packed brown sugar
1 teaspoon vanilla extract
3 cups old-fashioned rolled oats

1 cup semisweet or dark chocolate chips
½ cup peanut butter

Line an 8- or 9-inch square baking dish with parchment paper. Make sure an inch of paper hangs over the edges so that the bars can be lifted out more easily when they are done. (For thinner bars, use a parchment paper–lined 13 x 9-inch pan instead.)

In a large saucepan over medium heat, warm butter and brown sugar until the butter has melted and the sugar has dissolved. Stir in the vanilla extract. Mix in the oats. Cook over low heat for 3 to 4 minutes, or until ingredients are well blended.

Pour half the oat mixture into the prepared baking dish. Spread the mixture evenly, pressing down with your fingers as needed. Reserve the other half of the oat mixture for the second layer.

To make the filling, melt the chocolate chips and peanut butter together in a small saucepan over low heat and stir until smooth. Reserve about ¼ cup of the chocolate mixture for drizzling. Pour the rest of the chocolate mixture over the crust in the pan and spread evenly.

Pour the remaining oat mixture over the chocolate layer, pressing it in gently. Drizzle the top with the remaining chocolate mixture.

Refrigerate at least 2 to 3 hours, or overnight. Bring to room temperature before cutting into bars.

Note: Like any no-bake cookies, the final texture depends on how long you cook the sugar mixture. If you don't cook the sugar mixture long enough before adding the oats, the cookie/bar mixture will be soft; if you cook it too long, it could turn out dry and crumbly.

CHOCOLATE PEANUT BUTTER ROLL

Makes 12 to 16 servings

This is similar to my Pumpkin Roll (p. 173), but it features chocolate flavor instead of pumpkin. If you prefer chocolate to pumpkin, this is a great recipe to try.

Cake

4 large eggs, at room temperature

2 cups powdered sugar

¾ cup granulated sugar

½ teaspoon salt

1 tablespoon vanilla extract

⅔ cup all-purpose flour

⅓ cup cocoa powder

1¼ teaspoons baking powder

¼ cup vegetable or canola oil

6 tablespoons buttermilk

Filling

¾ cup heavy cream

⅔ cup plus ¾ cup powdered sugar, divided

⅔ cup creamy peanut butter

½ cup (1 stick) butter, softened to room temperature

Prepare cake: Preheat the oven to 350°F. Whisk eggs in a large bowl until frothy. Whisk in powdered and granulated sugars, salt, and vanilla until well blended. In a separate bowl, sift together flour, cocoa powder, and baking powder, then fold into the egg mixture. In a liquid measuring cup, whisk together the oil and buttermilk; stir into the chocolate mixture. Pour cake batter into a parchment paper–lined 15 x 10-inch jelly roll pan and bake at 350°F for 10 to 15 minutes, or until cake springs back when touched. Remove pan from oven and place on a wire rack for a few minutes.

Sprinkle a clean kitchen towel with powdered sugar. After cake has cooled slightly, flip cake over onto the prepared towel. Roll up the cake and towel and let cool completely.

Make filling: Whisk heavy cream until frothy in a large bowl, then gradually add ⅔ cup powdered sugar. Continue whisking until soft peaks form. Set aside.

In a separate bowl, whip peanut butter and butter together until light and fluffy. Add the remaining ¾ cup powdered sugar all at once and blend well. Fold in whipped cream mixture.

Unroll cooled chocolate cake, remove the kitchen towel, and spread the peanut butter filling evenly over cake. Roll cake back up, slice, and serve. Store leftover cake in the refrigerator.

EASY CHOCOLATE PEANUT BUTTER COOKIES

Makes 16 to 18 cookies

This simple recipe was given to me by one of my readers. It comes together easily and is a tasty, very soft cookie for those who love peanut butter.

1 cup creamy peanut butter
1 cup packed brown sugar
¼ cup all purpose flour
¼ cup (½ stick) melted butter
1 egg, beaten
1 teaspoon baking soda
1 cup mini chocolate chips

Preheat the oven to 350°F.

In a large bowl, mix together peanut butter, brown sugar, flour, melted butter, egg, baking soda, and mini chocolate chips. For better results, chill dough before baking. Drop the dough by tablespoonfuls onto a greased baking sheet, then crisscross with a fork. Bake at 350°F for 10 minutes.

Feeding a Crowd
RECIPES FOR FAMILY AND COMMUNITY GATHERINGS

HAYSTACK DINNER

Base recipe makes 4 to 6 servings; multiply as needed

This dish is often served at singings for the youth or for a church evening meal. Some also serve this for a community benefit meal to help a family with medical bills.

1 sleeve crushed saltine crackers

3 cups cooked and salted rice, or ½ pound (8 ounces) spaghetti noodles, cooked

½ cup finely chopped onion

1 cup chopped green bell peppers

2 large tomatoes, chopped

¼ cup finely chopped hot peppers

1 to 2 cups crushed corn chips or nacho cheese chips

1 pound ground beef, browned and mixed with one 1-ounce packet taco seasoning

1 (15-ounce) jar cheese sauce, warmed

8 ounces (1 cup) sour cream

1 pint salsa (see Salsa, p. 96)

Ranch dressing, for serving

Adjust the amounts as needed for the number of people you will be serving. Assemble ingredients in separate bowls and plates. Build your haystack according to how hungry you are with whichever ingredients you prefer.

HAYSTACK BREAKFAST

Base recipe makes 4 to 6 servings; multiply as needed

This is the breakfast version of the Haystack Dinner on page 216. We often serve this for brunch at our Christmas gathering. We like to add diced little smokies and ham to the usual ingredients. Other items can be added if desired. Everyone brings a few of the ingredients to contribute to the meal. After everyone has finished eating, we layer all the leftover foods into a baking dish. The next morning, it makes an easy breakfast of leftovers for the ones who hosted Christmas.

8 ounces ham, diced

8 ounces little smokies or smoked sausage, diced

1 (20-ounce) bag shredded hash browns, fried

6 eggs, cooked and scrambled

½ cup finely chopped onion

6 strips bacon, fried and crumbled

½ cup chopped green bell pepper

2 large tomatoes, chopped and seeded

1 cup sliced fresh mushrooms

1 (2¼-ounce) can black or green olives, sliced

4 cups sausage gravy

¼ cup finely chopped hot peppers

1 (15-ounce) jar cheese sauce, warmed

1 pint salsa (see Salsa, p. 96)

Adjust the amounts as needed for the number of people you will be serving. Assemble ingredients in separate bowls and plates. Layer all or whichever ingredients you prefer on your plate and top with cheese sauce and salsa.

WEDDING BROCCOLI CAULIFLOWER SALAD

Makes 75 to 100 servings

This salad makes frequent appearances at weddings. The day before, the cooks will wash and chop up all the broccoli and cauliflower. They also fry and crumble the bacon, shred the cheese, and mix the dressing. Assembling the salad on the day of the wedding is much simpler thanks to prepping the ingredients the day before.

4 heads broccoli
4 heads cauliflower
2 pounds bacon, fried and crumbled
2¼ pounds cheddar cheese, shredded

Dressing
7 cups sour cream
7 cups whipped salad dressing
1 cup ranch dressing
2⅔ cups granulated sugar
1⅓ teaspoons salt

Prepare the salad: Chop broccoli and cauliflower into small pieces and store in large containers. This should be done the day before the wedding (or before whatever event where you plan to serve the salad).

Prepare the dressing: In an extra-large mixing bowl, stir together ingredients and refrigerate. Several hours before serving, pour the dressing evenly over the cauliflower and broccoli mixture and stir together to make one batch. Refrigerate the salad until ready to serve.

GREEN BEANS WITH CHEESE SAUCE

Makes about 50 servings

We often prepare this for weddings, but our family loves it anytime, so I also make it quite often for family dinners. We purchase premixed Greek seasoning at the store, but you can make your own using a combination of ingredients like dried oregano, basil, parsley, dill, rosemary, thyme, garlic powder, onion powder, and salt and pepper.

8 quarts cooked or canned and drained green beans

Cheese sauce
1 cup (2 sticks) butter
2 pounds process cheese spread
1 cup milk
3 teaspoons Greek seasoning (see note above)
3 teaspoons black pepper
1 teaspoon seasoned salt

Cracker crumbs
15 sleeves round buttery crackers (do not remove from sleeves)
1¾ cups (3½ sticks) butter

Prepare the beans and cheese sauce: Place green beans in a large roasting pan. In a large pot or saucepan over low heat, stir together cheese sauce ingredients until melted. Pour cheese sauce over beans in the roasting pan and heat at 300°F until the beans are bubbling and heated through.

Prepare the cracker crumbs: Use your hands to crush the crackers while they are still in the plastic sleeves. Melt butter in a large skillet over medium heat, then add the cracker crumbs and toast them in the butter. Garnish individual servings of green beans with ½ cup toasted cracker crumbs right before serving.

BROWN BUTTER NOODLES

Makes 4 to 6 servings

These noodles are sometimes served as a side dish at weddings instead of Chicken Noodles (see p. 223). I have scaled it down significantly for preparing it at home. This is a dry noodle dish. Even without a sauce, these noodles have good flavor thanks to the brown butter. Watch the butter closely so it doesn't burn!

1 pound egg noodles
½ cup (1 stick) butter
Salt and pepper, to taste

Cook and drain noodles according to the package directions. To make brown butter: Melt butter in a saucepan over medium-low heat, stirring occasionally with a rubber spatula. The butter will start to bubble and foam. The milk solids will sink to the bottom of the pan and begin to turn brown. As soon as the butter smells nutty and toasted, turns a deep golden brown, and quits foaming, remove the pan from heat.

Pour the brown butter over cooked noodles and stir. Add salt and a little pepper to taste.

CHICKEN NOODLES

Makes one (20-gallon) canner full

This dish is served at weddings, funerals, and church meals. Sometimes chicken noodles are also made to serve with a benefit meal.

1 pound (4 sticks) butter
1 gallon (twelve 10½-ounce cans) cream of chicken soup
5 quarts chicken broth with meat (1 cup meat per quart)
2 cups chicken base
5 pounds uncooked egg noodles
3 cups diced and cooked potatoes
1½ cups chopped onion
1½ cups dried celery flakes
Salt, to taste
3 pounds process cheese spread, melted

Make the brown butter: Melt butter over medium-low heat in a small skillet. Stir occasionally with a rubber spatula. The butter will start to bubble and foam. The milk solids will sink to the bottom of the pan and begin to turn brown. As soon as the butter smells nutty and toasted, turns a deep golden brown, and stops foaming, remove the skillet from heat. Set butter aside.

In a 20-gallon canner or other extra-large pot, combine cream of chicken soup, chicken broth with meat, and chicken base. Fill the canner three-quarters full of water. Bring to a boil. When the mixture is boiling, add the noodles, potatoes, onions, and celery flakes. Season with salt to taste. Bring to a boil again, then remove from heat. Let stand for 30 minutes. Add cheese spread and brown butter and stir well to combine.

LOSS AND NEW LIFE

When a loved one dies, the grief is so hard to bear. I don't know how we would handle it without God, the church, friends, and family to support us.

In our community, everyone pitches in to make the load lighter for the family. As soon as word spreads across the community of a death in our churches, people come to help clean and prepare for the visitation and funeral. The men and boys clean the barns and outdoor area, set up tents, place the bench wagons around, and set up portable toilets for the crowds in the next few days. A walk-in cooler is brought in for the food. If needed, a portable cook kitchen will be brought in as well. A few men and women are put in charge to keep everything organized.

The women in charge will shop for groceries, if necessary, and get the food trays, plasticware, and coffee set up. They will call around asking other women to bring a casserole, salad, or dessert for the visitation meals. They also fill out slips of papers for the funeral food, and at the visitation, women will choose one to take home and make whatever is on the slip, such as a gallon of potato salad, a cake delight dessert, or several jars of chicken broth to prepare other dishes. Enough food is usually prepared for around five hundred people, though it might vary depending on the size of the family of the deceased. On the first evening, the church members of that district will come for supper and then sing for the family as people file through for the viewing. The second night, the youth group will come to sing.

We have had several visitations and funerals here at home for close family members, including after the passing of our son-in-law Mose. I will never forget when the youth sang "How Far Is Heaven" at the visitation. There wasn't a dry eye in the building.

After Mose's death, I hurt for my daughter Susan and her two young children. There were so many unanswered questions, so we turn it over to our heavenly Father, as we know he never makes a mistake. Someday we'll understand it all.

—*Lovina*

I always heard the saying "Life can change in a blink of an eye." It never really dawned on me how true that is till I lost my dear first husband, Mose. Without him, the sunniest days were dimmed too. He was the one I shared my deepest feelings with, the one I turned to when things seem hard. He loved our two dear children. He was willing to do anything for the children and me to make sure we were safe and happy.

Mose was in an automobile accident on his way to work one morning. His friend Dan was driving. A car crossed the center line and hit Dan's car head on. Dan was killed instantly. Mose hung on to life for five days before he passed away. We never got to say goodbye. My life felt like it ended with his. Our two little children, Jennifer (then age two) and Ryan (then age one), kept me going, along with plenty of support from family and friends.

Life doesn't stop even when it feels like it has. Everyone grieves differently, and we slowly move on. A year and five months after Mose passed, I met Ervin, a widower with three young children. Ervin had lost his dear first wife, Sarah, to cancer three months before I lost Mose.

God had plans for our future that we never thought would be possible. At first, it felt as if I was being unfaithful to Mose to let my heart love someone else. It was a challenge for Ervin and I and our five sweet children to become one family. But with God, anything is possible. God is love! And with the help of many peoples' prayers and our trust in God, we got married. We are now a blended family. Like any other family, we have our good and bad days. Recently, we added a sweet little baby, Ervin Jay, to our family, making a total of six children. God blesses us every day.

—Daughter Susan

CHICKEN PASTA CASSEROLE FOR A CROWD

Makes 25 to 30 servings

This is a very easy casserole to make when you are having a lot of company. I like to store diced, cooked chicken in my freezer to make it even easier to prepare a dish like this at a moment's notice.

1 teaspoon salt

2 pounds macaroni pasta

4 cups (or more) diced cooked chicken

2 (10½-ounce) cans cream of mushroom soup

2 (10½-ounce) cans cream of chicken soup

3¾ cups milk

2 pounds process cheese spread, cubed

In an 8-quart or larger stockpot, bring a full pot of water to a boil. Add salt and macaroni; cook the noodles until tender (check package instructions). Remove from heat and drain the water from the noodles. Add the rest of the ingredients to the pot and mix thoroughly with the cooked noodles, then pour into an 18- or 20-quart roasting pan. Bake at 350°F until heated thoroughly, about 1 hour.

GOURMET POTATOES

Makes 50 to 75 servings

This is another excellent recipe to make if you have a lot of guests; it offers meat and potatoes all in one dish. This can be divided into two roasting pans if you don't have a large enough roasting pan, which will also help the dish heat through faster. We typically use Club crackers.

1¾ pound (7 sticks) butter, divided
20 pounds potatoes, peeled, cubed, and cooked
8 pounds ham, cubed
2½ pounds (40 ounces) sour cream
3 pounds process cheese spread, cubed
6 (10½-ounce) cans cream of chicken soup
1 quart (4 cups) milk
Garlic salt, to taste
1½ pounds rectangular buttery crackers, crushed
Salt and pepper, to taste

Melt 1 pound (4 sticks) butter in the bottom of a large roasting pan. Add potatoes, ham, sour cream, process cheese spread, soup, and milk, mixing well. Sprinkle with a little garlic salt for extra flavor.

In a separate saucepan, melt the remaining ¾ pound (3 sticks) butter and stir in the crushed crackers. Season with salt and pepper. Sprinkle crackers over the potatoes. Bake at 350°F for 1½ hours, or until heated thoroughly.

OUTDOOR STEW FOR FIFTY

Makes enough for 50 adults

If you are having a large gathering in the summertime, this is a filling soup to make over a campfire. My husband, Joe, enjoys cooking outdoors on his fire pit that came with a kettle hook and grill.

4 pounds bacon, cut into 1-inch squares

8 pounds ground beef

3 pounds pork breakfast sausage

5 pounds smoky links, cut up

10 quarts chunked potatoes (1-inch pieces)

2 quarts chopped carrots (½-inch pieces)

2 quarts chopped celery (½-inch pieces)

1 quart chopped onion (½-inch pieces)

1 head cabbage, shredded

2 large green peppers, cut into ½-inch pieces

2 pounds frozen peas

Salt and pepper, to taste

Steak seasoning (optional)

Heat a 16- or 20-quart stewpot over an open fire. When the pot is warm enough that a drop of water sizzles, add the bacon. When enough grease collects at bottom to keep ingredients from sticking, add all the remaining meat. Cook, stirring occasionally, until the meat is mostly cooked through, then add the vegetables and enough water to cover. Cook the stew until the vegetables are soft, stirring regularly. Season to taste with salt and pepper and steak seasoning, if desired.

MIXED FRUIT

Makes about 300 servings

Mixed Fruit is often served at weddings. This recipe can be customized to your liking or with whatever fruit is in season. For example, the strawberries can be omitted in the winter. Reserve some of the grape slices and pineapple or other fruit to garnish the top.

20 quarts sliced peaches, drained (liquid may be reserved for glaze; may use fresh peaches instead if available)

24 fresh pineapples, cut into 1-inch chunks

15 pounds red seedless grapes, halved

10 pounds green seedless grapes, halved

2 quarts blueberries

6 yellow apples, peeled, cored, and sliced

6 red apples, peeled, cored, and sliced

2 quarts strawberries or additional chopped pineapple or halved grapes, for garnish (do not mix with other fruit)

3 (12-ounce) cans frozen orange juice concentrate, thawed (or use glaze option)

Divide all the fruit (except the strawberries or other fruit garnish) among three large (13-quart) mixing bowls. Add 1 can frozen orange juice concentrate to each bowl, or use the glaze option instead. Mix well.

Hull and cut strawberries into halves or quarters and place atop fruit in bowls. Alternatively, garnish with additional pineapple or grapes.

Glaze option

11 cups pineapple juice

11 cups water

3½ cups granulated sugar

3 cups instant Clear Jel thickened with 4 cups water

Pinch salt

1 (6-ounce) can frozen orange juice concentrate

¼ (12-ounce) can frozen lemonade concentrate

This glaze may be used instead of the frozen orange juice concentrate listed in the fruit recipe. In a large pot over medium heat, cook and stir the pineapple juice, water, sugar, Clear Jel mixture, and salt until thoroughly dissolved, then add orange juice and lemonade concentrate. Allow to cool, then pour the glaze over fruit. Make 3 gallons glaze for the Mixed Fruit recipe.

GRAPE SALAD FOR A CROWD

Makes about 40 servings

This is the perfect way to have your fruit and dessert all in one dish. We sometimes serve this dish at weddings. Since the recipe yields a large amount, it also works well to take to a potluck.

2½ (8-ounce) packages cream cheese (20 ounces), softened

5 cups sour cream

3¾ cups powdered sugar

¾ tablespoon freshly squeezed lemon juice

5 cups whipped topping

10 pounds seedless red and green grapes

2 (20-ounce) cans pineapple chunks, drained (optional)

Mix together cream cheese, sour cream, powdered sugar, lemon juice, and whipped topping. Fold in grapes and pineapple, if using. Keep refrigerated.

CAKE DELIGHT

Makes 24 servings

When someone in our Amish community passes away, the funeral committee will put slips of paper in a container at the viewing for people to take if they wish to help out with the meal after the funeral. Each slip has something written on it that the person will need to supply for the meal, such as several quarts of chicken broth, a gallon of potato salad, or a cake delight like this one. Everyone chooses whatever cake flavor or pie filling they want to use in this recipe so there is a variety.

1 (15- to 16-ounce) box cake mix (any flavor) plus necessary ingredients per package instructions

1½ (8-ounce) packages cream cheese (12 ounces), softened

12 ounces whipped topping, thawed slightly

½ cup powdered sugar

1½ quarts Homemade Fruit Pie Filling (p. 112), any flavor(s)

Preheat oven to 350°F.

Prepare cake mix batter according to package directions. Pour into a greased 15 x 10-inch jelly roll pan and bake at 350°F for 20 to 25 minutes. Remove cake from oven and let cool.

In a large mixing bowl, cream together cream cheese, whipped topping, and powdered sugar. Spread the cream cheese mixture on cooled cake. Top with pie filling of your choice.

LIFE IN OUR CHURCH COMMUNITY

*O*ur community rotates hosting church services throughout the year. The services are held every other week at people's homes. Hosting church services is one way of ensuring a thorough cleaning of your house yearly. Of course, your house doesn't have to be spotless to hear God's Word, but it is a nice goal to have and the commitment helps to get all your cleaning done at once! The walls, ceilings, and floors are all washed, furniture and windows are cleaned as well, plus closets and cabinets are organized, and so on. We hold services in our pole barn when we host, so that is also cleaned thoroughly.

Next comes preparing the food for that day's midday meal. Our menu usually consists of homemade wheat and white bread, pickles, red beets, peanut butter spread, butter, jelly, and hot peppers. Most people will add ham, cheese, egg salad, or cheese spread to their menu. Coffee and tea and a variety of cookies are served too. Little bags of popcorn are passed out to everyone while the women wash dishes. The bread, cookies, and popcorn are all brought in by the women of the church. The clean dishes are kept in totes and packed back in the bench wagon that will be pulled to the next place that will host the service.

If a family doesn't have enough room to host in a heated building in the winter months, they will rent one of the church-owned tents during the summer months instead. Some host families will invite some or all the church families back to their home for supper; others will just invite their own family to stay or come back later. Some will not invite anyone to join them for an additional meal. Hosting is acceptable however someone is able to do it. Supper will usually be a haystack dinner (see my version on p. 216) or casseroles that are prepared the day before. Most times the salads and desserts are brought in by family members of the host.

Sometimes the singing for the youth is held where church was hosted earlier in the day. Youth ages sixteen and over attend the singing. The boys usually sit at one table and the girls at another. They all sit down to eat and then stay seated to sing. Singings are always on Sunday evenings. It's so enjoyable to sit down with the youth and sing with them. We also have a youth group called Labors of Love that helps a family once a month. The boys help with work such as fencing, cutting wood, and repairs around the house or

barn. The girls help with weeding gardens and flower beds, washing walls, and sometimes painting.

During the week, the church women sometimes gather for a coffee break with a new mother who has moved to the church with her family. It helps to welcome them and is a nice time to get better acquainted. The church women also gather for coffee breaks for each other's birthdays. Everyone brings a dish for these coffee breaks, and soon we have quite a variety of food. We also get together for knotting comforters and quilting.

Our church community comes together in other ways as well. When a family is in need because of hospital bills, community members will gather for fundraisers such as a sub sandwich, chicken, or fry pie drive. The men will also help out if someone needs help building a house or barn lost in a storm or fire.

Sometimes families move to another state or community. Before they move away, our church will host a potluck dinner in their honor to say good-bye. After supper we sing for them. It is always nice to be together.

—*Lovina*

MOCHA PUDDING

Makes 16 to 20 servings

This pudding is often served at weddings. It can be made the day before and frozen. Then it's taken out of the freezer in the morning so that it's thawed by lunchtime. Daughter Susan and new son-in-law Ervin had this for a dessert at their wedding. It is one of Ervin's favorites; he and Susan bring this a lot to family night when it's their turn to bring dessert. The mocha flavor comes from the combination of chocolate syrup and coffee concentrate.

2 cups crushed chocolate sandwich cookies (24 cookies)

3 tablespoons butter, melted

1 (8-ounce) package cream cheese, softened

1 teaspoon vanilla extract

1 (14-ounce) can sweetened condensed milk

1¼ teaspoon instant coffee mixed with 4¾ teaspoons water

½ cup chocolate syrup, plus additional for decorating

1 (16-ounce) container whipped topping, thawed slightly

1 (3.4-ounce) box vanilla instant pudding mix

2 cups milk

Mix the crushed cookies with the melted butter and press the mixture into the bottom of a 13 x 9-inch resealable plastic or glass container. In a separate bowl, whip the cream cheese until fluffy. Stir in the vanilla. Add the condensed milk a little at a time, mixing well each time. Add the coffee concentrate and chocolate syrup and mix again. Gently stir in the whipped topping.

In another bowl, mix the instant pudding with the milk. Then add the pudding mixture to the cream cheese mixture and combine well. Pour the cream cheese pudding mixture into the container on top of the cookie crust. Drizzle chocolate syrup from the top to the bottom of the pan. Swirl with a knife going the other direction. Refrigerate before serving.

CHERRY BARS FOR A CROWD

Makes about 3 dozen bars

This large recipe makes an excellent contribution to a potluck or holiday dinner.

1½ cups (3 sticks) butter, softened

3 cups granulated sugar

5 large eggs

1½ teaspoons salt

1½ teaspoons vanilla extract

1½ teaspoons almond extract

5½ cups all-purpose flour

1½ teaspoons baking powder

2 (21-ounce) cans cherry pie filling

Glaze

1 cup powdered sugar

3 tablespoons milk

Preheat the oven to 350°F. Line a 17 x 12-inch half sheet pan with aluminum foil. Spray with nonstick spray. Set aside.

In the bowl of a stand mixer, cream together butter and granulated sugar for 1 to 2 minutes. Add eggs, salt, vanilla, and almond extract, and continue stirring until fully incorporated. Add flour and baking powder and mix until just combined. Reserve 1¾ cups of dough to use as the topping. Spread and press the remaining dough into prepared baking pan.

Top the dough in the pan with cherry pie filling. Drop the remaining dough in small pieces over the pie filling. Bake for 50 to 60 minutes, or until the top is golden brown. Remove from the oven and place the pan on a wire rack to cool completely.

Prepare the glaze: In a medium bowl, whisk together powdered sugar and milk until smooth and drizzle over the cooled bars. Cut glazed bars into squares and serve.

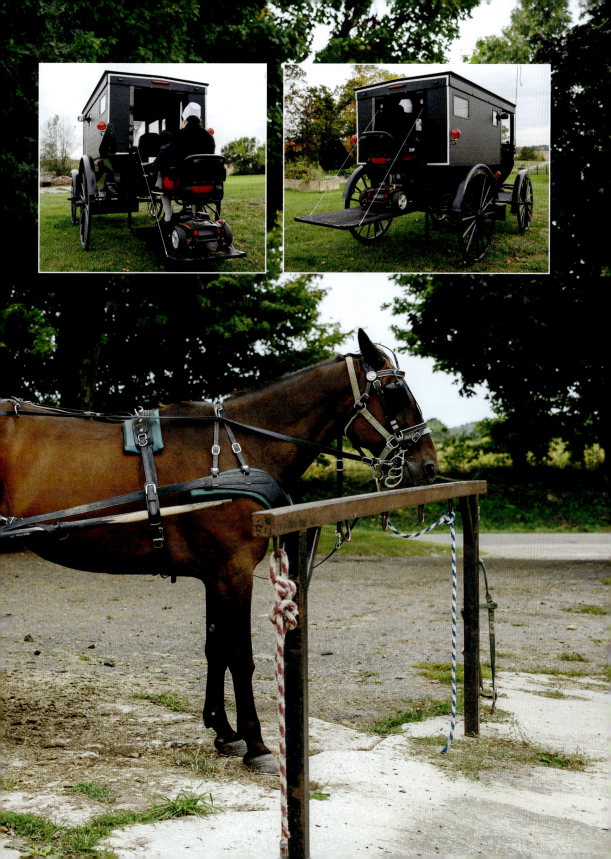

ACKNOWLEDGMENTS

Another cookbook is almost done and ready for press. Life has included many changes as we travel into the unknown future. During the process of making this book, two more grandbabies joined the family, we prepared for a wedding celebration, and hosted church services and several Christmas gatherings. Life brings so many changes, some happy, some sad. We have lost loved ones and gained new family members.

I want to thank my family for their support as I took time from my busy life to accomplish this book. Special thanks go to my husband of thirty-one years, Joe, and to my firstborn, Elizabeth (30), her husband Tim, and their children, Abigail Elizabeth, Timothy Josiah, Allison Lovina, and Andrea Ruby. To my daughter Susan (28), who has seen a lot of heartache in her young years and recently remarried after the loss of her first husband. Ervin and Susan have six children altogether and are a great blended family. Their children are Kaitlyn Rose, Jennifer Susan, Isaiah Edward, Ryan Isaiah, Curtis Dale, and Ervin Jay.

Thanks also to daughter Verena (26) and her special friend Daniel Ray. Verena recently moved back home after moving out three years ago to be with Susan and the children after our son-in-law Mose's death. She continued to live alone for a year after Susan remarried but is now back here at home, which I'm so glad for.

To son Benjamin (almost 25); and to daughter Loretta (almost 24) and her husband Dustin and their children, Denzel Michael and Byron Liam. To son Joseph (almost 22) and his special friend, Grace. To daughter Lovina (20) and her special friend, Daniel. By the time this book comes out, Daniel and Lovina will have joined hands in marriage, Lord willing. Lovina typed up all the recipes for me, which greatly helped. To son Kevin (18), who was a great recipe tester for all of these recipes. I think Joe and all the boys didn't mind having extra goodies in their lunches after a day of making recipes for the photography sessions.

A thank-you also goes to my editor Sara Versluis for being patient and understanding with me as I wrote this book piece by piece, and to all at Herald Press, namely Amy Gingerich, Elisabeth Ivey, Rachel E. Martens, Merrill Miller, Laura Leonard Clemens, LeAnn Hamby, Joe Questel, and Alyssa Bennett Smith. I'm always relieved when the book is off to press.

I would also like to thank the photographer and food stylist Jen (and her husband Grant) for extra consideration and being respectful of our religion while taking photos, which I'm sure wasn't always easy. We have become great friends through the process of making these books.

Thank you to all of you for helping in any way you could, including baking and photography days, writing pieces for this book, or just for being there and supporting me. I am so blessed to have a loving family and my love for them is so great.

As each of you travel through life, may God hold his protecting hand over you and shower you with his many blessings. Happy cooking!

INDEX

THE AUTHOR

Lovina Eicher is the author of *Amish Family Recipes*, *The Essential Amish Cookbook*, and several other cookbooks. She writes the popular syndicated column Lovina's Amish Kitchen, which appears in dozens of newspapers around the United States as well as on a Facebook page with over nine thousand followers. Lovina and her husband Joe have eight children and a growing number of grandchildren. They live in rural Michigan.